COMMONSENSE TIME MANAGEMENT

The WorkSmart Series

The Basics of Business Writing
Commonsense Time Management
How to Speak and Listen Effectively
Successful Team Building

COMMONSENSE TIME MANAGEMENT

ROY ALEXANDER

amacom
American Management Association
The WorkSmart Series

This book is available at a special
discount when ordered in bulk quantities.
For information, contact Special Sales Department,
AMACOM, a division of American Management Association,
135 West 50th Street, New York, NY 10020.

This publication is designed to provide accurate and authoritative information in regard to the subject matter covered. It is sold with the understanding that the publisher is not engaged in rendering legal, accounting, or other professional service. If legal advice or other expert assistance is required, the services of a competent professional person should be sought.

Library of Congress Cataloging-in-Publication Data

Alexander, Roy.
Commonsense time management / Roy Alexander.
p. cm. — (The WorkSmart series)
ISBN 0-8144-7791-7
1. Executives—Time management. I. Title. II. Series.
HD38.2.A57 1992
658.4'093—dc20 *91-41433*
CIP

Printing number

10 9 8 7 6

To
Ruth Upshaw Alexander

Her original reverence for finite resources inspired my zeal for time, the most priceless resource of all. Without her continuing inspiration, much of my time would have rendered out dross.

CONTENTS

Part III. Managing Time Wasters

Part IV. Controlling Your Tools

Part V. Taming Travel Time

PREFACE:

THE GAME OF BUSINESS SOLITAIRE

Think of time as a deck of cards. Each day you get a new deck with 52 cards (just as you get 24 hours each day)—no more, no less. It's up to you what you do with the cards. You cannot say you don't have enough cards (*time*) because that's all there are. No one gets more or less.

The game of business solitaire has no winners or losers—just opportunity to progress. Note we say *progress,* not reach *perfection.* Perfection encourages people to freeze up, unable to take action. This wastes time.

In laying out the cards, do your best at all times. But no matter what your skill or how advanced your zeal, the unexpected card (phone call, meeting, etc.) always turns up. How you handle the unexpected *within* the rules of the game is the rewarding part of time management.

Before you turn to Chapter 1, take a moment to take a diagnostic test—about you and time. It will help you pinpoint your strengths and weaknesses in managing time.

R.A.

ACKNOWLEDGMENTS

Primary recognition, of course, must go to the thousands of managers of time—some good in some ways, a favored few excellent in many ways.

When it comes to thanking individuals, the heroic services of Christine West in terrier-like research and Connie Jason in creative graphics cry out for recognition—hereby rendered. David Jackson and Enrique Pabon did word processing under conditions that make Rosetta stone translation look like kindergarten 101.

PART I

THINKING ABOUT TIME

DIAGNOSTIC TEST: YOU AND TIME

	Often	Sometimes	Rarely
1. Do you handle each piece of paperwork only once?	☐	☐	☐
2. Do you begin and finish projects on time?	☐	☐	☐
3. Do people know the best time to reach you?	☐	☐	☐
4. Do you do something every day that moves you closer to your long-range goals?	☐	☐	☐
5. When you are interrupted, can you return to your work without losing momentum?	☐	☐	☐
6. Do you deal effectively with long-winded callers?	☐	☐	☐
7. Do you focus on preventing problems before they arise rather than solving them after they happen?	☐	☐	☐
8. Do you meet deadlines with time to spare?	☐	☐	☐
9. Are you on time to work, to meetings, and to events?	☐	☐	☐
10. Do you delegate well?	☐	☐	☐
11. Do you write daily To–Do Lists?	☐	☐	☐
12. Do you finish all the items on your To–Do List?	☐	☐	☐
13. Do you update in writing your professional and personal goals?	☐	☐	☐
14. Is your desk clean and organized?	☐	☐	☐
15. Can you easily find items in your files?	☐	☐	☐
Subtotal	______	______	______
	×4	×2	×0
Total	______	______	______

What the Test Says About You

Give yourself 4 points for every *often* you checked. Give yourself 2 points for every *sometimes*. Give yourself 0 points for every *rarely*.

Add your points together and place yourself with the proper group:

49–60	You manage your time well. You are in control of most days and most situations.
37–48	You manage your time well some of the time. However, you need to be more consistent with time-saving strategies. Adding new techniques is allowed!
25–36	You are all too often a victim of time. Don't let each day manage you. Apply the techniques you learn here right away.
13–24	You are close to losing control. Probably too disorganized to enjoy quality time. A new priority-powered time plan is needed now!
0–12	You are overwhelmed, scattered, frustrated, and probably under a lot of stress. Put the techniques in this book into practice. Star chapters—for special study—that treat your problem areas.

CHAPTER 1

HOW TO THINK ABOUT TIME

"For tyme ylost may nought recovered be."

—CHAUCER

More than 600 years ago, Geoffrey Chaucer—en route to Canterbury—marveled that time (once lost) could never be recovered. Through the centuries, men and women have continued the quest for that "ineffable ineluctable essence" of time control. Consultant Peter Drucker, a modern tour guide whose destination is not Canterbury but the industrial park called Good Management, says grimly: "Time is the scarcest resource. Unless it is managed, nothing can be managed."

THE CONTRADICTIONS OF TIME

Yes, time can be managed, but not the way you manage other resources. In fact, "time management" may be a misconception. In many cases, time manages you.

Business is concerned with wise management of resources: capital, physical, human, information, and time. The first four can be manipulated. You can increase your work force, decrease it, or change its composition. With capital, you can increase it, save it, spend it, or hold steady. You can invest it in a new plant or use it to fund a branch office. If you need more, you can issue public stock, get a loan, or increase your product prices.

But time, the "ineffable resource," is unique. It is finite. There is only so much time, and no matter what you do, you can't get more. It's the only resource that must be spent (invested or wasted!) the instant you get it. And you must spend at one never-varying rate: 60 seconds per minute, 60 minutes per hour. No discounts, no inflation.

Thus, the very notion of time control is a paradox. For you can only manage *yourself* in relation to time. You cannot choose *whether* to spend it, but only *how*. Once you waste time, it's gone—and it cannot be replaced.

In fact, time was created by humankind as a convenience—an expensive convenience when you buy it from someone else. In Florida a man bills his doctor $90 for keeping him waiting. In New York a woman pays someone $20 an hour to do her shopping—out of a catalogue. For $1,500 you can have a fax machine put in your car, alongside your cellular phone.

What has all this gained us? Not more time. We already know there isn't any more. Not more freedom. If you pay someone to pick up your laundry while you stay late at the office, you're only trading one chore for another.

But do not despair. Time management techniques can save you at least an hour a day, probably two. But the real question is, will you use those two extra hours to good advantage?

Time is the basic stuff of the universe. Most people feel they're wasting barrels of this irreplaceable commodity. They're right. Good management of time is probably the single most important factor in managing yourself, your work, and indeed the work of others. Once you stop trying to wrestle time to the ground, its grip on you eases. Don't try to "conquer" time. Work with it. Make it your friend.

Time management, like other management disciplines, responds to analysis and planning. To place yourself on good terms with time, you must know what problems you encounter in applying it wisely, and what causes those problems. From this base you can improve your effectiveness in and around time.

Time management, a personal process, must fit your style and circumstances. Changing old habits requires strong commitment; however, if you choose to apply the principles, you can obtain the rewards.

Where is the best place to begin digging into priority-oriented time management? Check the ways you control time available to you now. No one has total control over a daily schedule. Someone or something always makes demands. However, you have as much control as anyone else—and probably more than you realize. Even within structured time you have opportunities to select *which* tasks to handle at *what* priorities. In exercising your discretionary choices, you begin to control your time.

TIME: ENIGMA WRAPPED IN RIDDLE

Probably everyone alive today has said: "I would if I had the time," or, "There just isn't enough time," or, "Someday, I'll do that when I have time." The idea is widespread that people are about to run out of time. But that just isn't true. It's a paradox. Although time is not in short supply, it must be rationed.

Consider the supply question. Your basic truth about supply is this: You have as much time as Methuselah had. He had just 24 hours a day, just as you do. Moreover, no one since Methuselah has been richer in time than you. Further, time's distribution would delight the most zealous egalitarian. It never discriminates regardless of sex, sect, station, or degree. So worrying about the supply of time is pointless. The supply has never been better.

Then why this need to ration a commodity every person has in full measure? For one reason—Different rules apply to two classes of time: (1) time that's under your personal control, and (2) time you've contracted to another for pay.

ON YOUR OWN TIME

Your own time is not nearly as scarce as widespread wailing indicates. Say you work 40 hours a week for nearly 49 weeks per year (52 weeks less 2 weeks of vacation and 6 holidays). In a year your work time comes to 1,952 hours. Deduct that from your total inventory of time—8,760 (365 × 24) hours a year. Then deduct 488 hours traveling to and from your job; 1,095 hours for meals (3 hours a day every day of the year); another hour each day for dressing and undressing: 365 hours; and 8 hours' sleep a night—count 2,920 hours for that. Your total deduction: 6,820 hours. Subtract 6,820 from 8,760 and you get 1,940 hours to do as you please. That's nearly 81 days of 24 hours apiece, 22 percent of the entire year!

(Text continues on page 10.)

TIME LAB
Q&A ON EFFECTIVENESS

Q. Isn't good time management at bottom what you'd expect from any *efficient* person?

A. To be efficient is to use the fewest resources for a given task. Effectiveness is a function of goal accomplishment (either you reach your objective or you don't). Many people become quite efficient doing things that don't need to be done in the first place. Determine first what you should be doing. Then ask how it can be done most efficiently. Do the *right* things *right.*

Q. Sure, I see using time management for important tasks. Isn't that enough without all the small stuff, too?

A. Day-to-day activities need the *most* planning. Keep a daily time record. Identify the patterns. Use this information in scheduling. Emphasize early actions. As the morning goes, so does the day. Recall the old pol's axiom: "As Maine goes, so goes the nation."

Q. You tell me to work on priorities. But *they* won't let me!

A. You must control not only priorities but *them* (whoever they are). When tempted to deviate from your plan, ask: "Is what I am *about* to do more important than what I *planned* to do?" If more important, go right ahead. If not (usually the case), look for ways to postpone, reschedule, or delegate.

Q. Can't most competent managers identify their biggest time wasters?

A. Without a system, it's hard. Try reconstructing last week—you'll see. Habits are automatic. Your time patterns often become inconsistent with what you're trying to accomplish. Most managers waste at least two hours every day but don't know where.

Keep a time log. Determine where time is being wasted. You'll be surprised!

Q. I'd like to get time organized, I really would. But won't I then miss out on spontaneous opportunities?

A. Priority-powered managers believe in planned spontaneity. Once you're on top of things, take Wednesday morning off. Do whatever strikes your fancy. Schedule fun in your life. Manage activities better so you gain more time to do other things you enjoy.

Good time management means *decreasing* marginal commitments and *increasing* true priorities.

Q. Isn't writing out objectives a waste of time? I could be *doing*—not scribbling.

A. Writing out your plan is always a good investment. ("If you don't know where you're going, you'll get there in a hurry!") Too often mental notes are vague and ill defined. You won't forget written goals. Writing increases commitment. The greater your commitment, the more likely your accomplishment.

Q. Can't most managers find many ways to *save* time on their own?

A. Yes, to some extent. But your need is to *invest* time. There is no way to save time. It

(continues)

cannot be banked for the future. All time is real time. It must all be utilized now. Waste it. Or invest it. The choice is yours.

Q. My astrological sign is inconsistent with being organized. Doesn't that mean I'm hopeless with time control?

A. To priority-activate time is to take action on purpose instead of settling for random selection. We're sure you're kidding about your horoscope. Your own free will is the critical element.

Is this so niggardly you'd file a formal complaint? "Maybe not," you demur. "Still it's not enough. Look at all the things I can't get done because there isn't time!"

"Far from being overwhelmed with things to do, you're simply indecisive about selecting *ways* to fill those hours," the skeptic might say. But who better than you to say whether your own time problem is (1) too many demands, or (2) too many options? Either way, the solution is *better management of time*.

FIRST THINGS FIRST

In this book you'll learn to set long-range goals in both personal and professional arenas. Then, working backward, you'll plan successively shorter range objectives. Each is a specific target with a deadline; taken one at a time, each will lead you toward one of your long-range goals.

Next, you'll learn about setting priorities and you'll practice a technique for rank ordering your activities. These two building blocks serve as a foundation for planning your time. The third part of the system concerns block time allocated to key task categories. Other steps are built on these three. But first, in Chapter 2, you're scheduled to take a field trip—to watch time managers at work.

CHAPTER 2

IN THE FIELD: HOW TIME MANAGERS MAKE IT WORK

"Time, gentlemen, time! Time, gentlemen, time!"

—BRITISH PUB OWNERS' TRADITIONAL CLOSING CRY

Following an in-company seminar, the time consultant walked through the office to discover one of his attendees breaking a cardinal rule—answering his own telephone!

"I hope you're following the *other* advisories better than that," the consultant said, half-serious, half-banter.

"Story of my life, Dr. Stevenson. Made A on the lecture, F on the fieldwork."

Before you get into the *science* of time management, take a trip to the field. Watch inventive time managers wrestle with what Shakespeare called "the clock-setter, that bald sexton, time." Then, as you dig into the science of time-walloping, you'll see the principles these deft managers are drawing on.

WHY MEHDI SAYS NOTHING'S IMPOSSIBLE

Mehdi Fakarzadah came to the United States from the Middle East. He knew no one. Against all odds, he took a job selling insurance for MetLife. In a few years, he had become a millionaire and outsold everyone on MetLife's 20,000-person sales force. One of his secrets: priority-oriented time management.

Mehdi—an enormously successful insurance salesman—is also an astute investor of time. He carefully orchestrates his primary selling time days and weeks in advance.

"Each person is created equal to every other person in the matter of time," Mehdi says. "We each get 24 hours per day. What we each do with that 24 hours makes a vast difference in what we accomplish."

If you manage your time so you save 1 hour per day, Mehdi says, you've created 365 new hours for yourself in one year alone. That's equivalent to nine 40-hour workweeks. Imagine the value of nine extra weeks. More effective work, more enjoyable leisure!

"We live an average of 600,000 hours," Mehdi says. "We sleep 200,000 hours and work 200,000 hours. We spend about 25,000 hours educating ourselves, 75,000 in recreation, and 100,000 hours in various other personal affairs."

In short, only one-third of our time on earth provides for ourselves and our families. Each work hour then must provide for two other nonwork hours.

Effective use of time is crucial for Mehdi because he collects *only when the prospective buyer signs the agreement.*

"Selling is like chopping wood," Mehdi says. "You must do many things to get ready to chop wood. But only the actual chopping really counts. You must prepare the workplace, walk to the woodpile, select a log, return to the workplace, position the log, raise the axe, split the wood, pick up the pieces, then return to the woodpile to repeat the cycle. Which action is truly significant? Splitting the wood, of course.

"If you don't split the wood, there's no point in the rest. If you can figure a way to split the wood without the other activities, you still have the achievement. Actual time the blade is spent splitting the log is less than 2 percent of the total job time. Most of your time is spent getting ready or following through."

Mehdi's time management philosophy sounds almost too simple until you realize how many people overlook the obvious: "I decide what I want to do," he says. "I lay out plans for doing it. And I do it quickly."

Scientific Scheduling

The key to successful time management is making a conscious decision to achieve a specific goal. Mehdi begins the day early; is out of bed by 5:30 A.M., exercises to keep physically fit and to maintain energy. After cooking his own breakfast ("Never omit breakfast. It's not healthy!") he leaves for his midtown Manhattan office. He starts work between 7:00 and 7:30 A.M.

Before traditional hours begin at 9:00 A.M., Mehdi has completed his paperwork for the day. When co-workers start coming into the office, he's ready for the meetings and telephone calls. He controls these events to his liking: Only those that deserve priority selling time get it.

He keeps 9:00 A.M. to 5:00 P.M. free for prospect meetings—including lunch hour. After 5:00 P.M. Mehdi goes back on secondary time to wrap up loose ends. He leaves for home between 6:00 and 7:00 P.M.

As well organized as each day is, it all conforms to a larger plan built around his annual sales goal—established every January. In November he evaluates his progress toward the goal. Usually it's in reach. But with year's end approaching, he'll drop everything to make sure he achieves his objective.

When the goal becomes all-consuming, priorities order themselves naturally. If he reaches a goal earlier than planned, he sets a new goal—higher. He *must* have a goal.

Any activity that doesn't relate to a sale he delegates to Ike, his administrative assistant. (Mehdi keeps his eye on the main chance.) When he ended up with a free half day prior to a speaking engagement, Mehdi asked the program director: "Do you know a corporation president?" "Yes," John Hill responded curiously. "Why?" "I want to see him," Mehdi said.

"Well," Hill said, "I wrote a $100,000 policy for Jack Francis a few years ago. He owns a small electronics company. I haven't been able to sell him anything since. But I'll tell him you're a famous speaker in town for a special conference. He'd probably be interested in meeting you. But you'll never make a sale."

John Hill called Francis, who reluctantly agreed to meet. Mehdi talked to him about a deferred compensation plan covering his key employees. Before Mehdi went on the platform that afternoon, he had virtually wrapped up a $1.5 million sale. He had turned a dead time into opportunity.

Goal Setting

Mehdi sees success tied to the goal-setting part of time management. He recommends:

- *Step one.* List the life goals most important to you: family, salary, spouse, golf game, personal development, business achievement. When everything's down, re-list in order of importance.
- *Step two.* Estimate time spent on these major goals. Then follow up. Keep an activities log. Is time proportionate to the priority of each goal?

The value of goal managing is backed by hard fact. A major university studied alumni 20 years after graduation. Only 3 percent had established clear lifetime aims, monitored their activities to suit these aims, and occasionally made appropriate modifications. This 3 percent had accomplished more than the others. In short, individuals with clear-cut goals are much more likely to leave permanent footprints.

At first, you'll find glaring discrepancies between goal importance and time orientation. Most people spend less than 15 percent of their time on priority items. Double the 15 to a mere 30 percent and you're miles ahead. The richest payoff comes when life goals are the foundation for minute-to-minute actions. It's worth working on.

To improve time-to-goal rating, Mehdi recommends:

- *Use pruning shears.* Trim activities that contribute little to life goals. When you spot an activity with virtually no priority, lop it off. If a needed area takes too much time, chop time allotted in half. Warning: Don't save time on one thing to squander it on a task equally wasteful. Ask yourself: "Is this a priority project?"—before, during, and after. Soon you'll be screening out low-value activities with little conscious effort.

• *Allow for one planning hour a day.* It can save three implementation hours. That's power!

• *Avoid incompletion.* Answer a letter when you read it. Each time you pick up an unfinished job, you waste time getting started/remembering/covering old ground. Memory is useful, but free your energy for better uses.

• *Delegate routine work.* The more productive you are, the more your boss wants to free you of detail—to make more time for what *only you* can do.

WHEN PRIORITIES GO AWRY

At one printing company, Saskatchewan consultant Alan Scharf relates, the sales force always discovered itself behind

---

TIME NUGGETS: CLASSIC PRINCIPLES OF TIME CONTROL

The principles of effective management of work time are well established:

- ***Make a list.*** **Nothing ever gets done until it gets on a list of things to do—and perhaps not then. But once there *is* a list, everything has a chance.**
- ***Assign priorities.*** **What should be done first? Second? What can wait? Arrange items on your list in order of importance.**
- ***Do first things first.*** **Top priority matters most, for reasons you yourself have determined.**
- ***Brook no interruptions.*** **If you are truly serious, not even a telephone offer of a free pest inspection will deter you. Moreover, you probably won't even answer the phone.**
- ***Keep at item one until time runs out.*** **Resume work on it the instant time becomes available again. It always does.**
- ***Work item one until you finish with it.*** **Then start item two, now your new item one.**

---

quota by the third week of each month. They'd coast for the first three weeks, get behind, then sell like crazy to make monthly quota. They worked hard during the first part of each month on preparation, not selling. They sold only one week each month.

Once the manager recognized that only the selling brought in money, he hired more office help. His sales doubled in one year and his profits tripled. His salespeople spent more time *actually selling*. Here good time management was also good management (often the case).

One small manufacturing company was just breaking even on sales of $70,000 per year. The new general manager, formerly sales manager, spent most of his time doing "administrative work" (translation: moving papers around). Sure, he kept in touch with old customers he'd known for years—yet the company averaged 8 percent customer loss per year. Things were getting tougher and tougher. The GM hired an office manager and went out selling three mornings a week. Sales increased by $30,000. Priorities had been aligned. He hired a general manager to work for him.

Comprehensive Time Management

Barry Glick, CEO of Almost Heaven, Inc., Rennick, West Virginia, sees priority-driven time management "as a journey. New side roads keep materializing as we go along."

One recent side road: fax. "Five years ago," Glick says, "the time-control traveler would've said to fax: 'Huh?' Today you say: 'Of course.' But we've had to relearn time effectiveness to get *best* use (not *overuse*—always a peril with a new tool) for the fax."

Astute managers must hone their time management skills each day, since "there's not enough time available for even an expert time manager like me," Glick says, wryly. The good time manager is an orchestra conductor—harmonizing six to ten instruments to achieve a unified effect, Glick believes.

"In my time orchestra, the most active instruments are *delegating, screening calls* (and training employees to make both happen), and a mechanical synthesizer called outbound WATS. An outbound WATS line saves time and money and pays off in relaxation time," Glick says, luxuriating in one of his own hot tubs. "You can't beat that combo."

Glick is perceptive about what *not* to delegate. "Here I do all the insect killing on a do-it-yourself basis," he says, swatting a fly. (He's kidding. Or is he?)

The Daily Work Map

Careerist mothers find work–home priorities on the same list: *Meet with the advertising director, complete company budget report, pick up Joey from Little League.*

How do you keep track of everything—and get it all done? Each manager follows his or her own path to efficiency, but most agree on the staple of time management: the To–Do List (see Chapter 3).

Susan Stautberg operates New York–based MasterMedia Limited. Her three-and-a-half-year-old business (sales of $600,000 last year) has a catalogue of 31 books, including two Literary Guild selections, and represents 150 speakers. At any one time, Stautberg is promoting current books, preparing catalogue copy for upcoming releases, and making plans to acquire new books. She also is a class mother at her son's school.

A typical day is punctuated by endless phone calls and meetings. "My To–Do List keeps me on course," she says. She prepares her list at day's end from paper scraps she's scribbled notes on—including phone calls yet unreturned, play dates for her son, and reminders (*take tomorrow's dinner out of freezer*).

Evenings at home she adds on other items that come to mind. Next morning, at the office, Stautberg and her assistant go over "must-do's" for the day.

Stautberg keeps her To–Do List on a pad that fits into various binders "traveling with me everywhere." Business items go on the left, prioritized A and B; personal items go on the right. Under *Business,* she lists key books in the works—then notes next steps: *Call author, set up promotion meeting.* After the first steps she adds follow-up steps (*set speaking dates, notify Tony*).

She breaks down large projects, like planning a media tour, into bite-size tasks—*make travel arrangements, book speaking*—entered on a specific day's list.

"Crossing off small chunks gives me a sense of progress toward my goal," she says. The To–Do List, although a valuable guide, isn't a dictator. Stautberg builds unplanned time into her list. "I use unexpected five minutes to call home, set up business meetings, outline a speech, or just stare into space and recharge," she says. "I never let the list get out of hand. I stick to one page per day."

Linking priority tasks to peak energy also helps organize schedules for maximum efficiency. Body biorhythms studies suggest that each person functions better at some times of the day than others.

"Think about when your daily energy is highest and try to match high-priority tasks to your peak energy hours," suggests Ann McGee-Cooper of Dallas, Texas. "For instance, if you're not a morning person, devote earlier hours to low-priority tasks, such as sorting mail and returning phone calls."

Time-Saving Tips From Executives

And still they come, no two alike, from all work groups and situations, all in pursuit of priority-oriented time management:

- A corporate financial planner: "I used to spend hours agonizing over tough decisions. Then I realized that hesitation rarely made for a better decision. Now I just gather the facts, then decide quickly. My track record is as good as ever. And I have time for other important matters."
- A corporate troubleshooter: "When I step into an ailing company, I look for ways to put its best resources up against its toughest problems. For example, I put each executive in charge of solving a single critical problem. This combination of concentration and pressure usually leads to top results in record time."
- A bank executive: "I never watched the clock and usually kept staff people waiting 15 minutes or longer to see me. As a result, the people felt insulted and lost loyalty. Now I keep

staff appointments to the minute. Employees have become more loyal. They work harder as well."

• The administrator of a medical center: "Good relationships with staff are important, but the usual social chatter can take too much time. Instead of trying to socialize with everyone, each day I give a different person my full attention for several minutes."

• The chief executive of a large retailer: "I had scheduling problems until I learned the swift task/slow task concept. Now I do swift tasks, like making quick decisions or delegating, during fragmented times of the day. I put slow tasks, like drafting reports or looking at a complex deal, into consecutive-hour time slots, when I can make real progress."

• The president of a bank: "I schedule my work sessions for 90 minutes at a time. That's as long as I can productively concentrate on one project. After each session, I catch up on calls and messages that have piled up. The routine break refreshes me, and soon I'm ready for another work session."

• An industrial consultant: "I can predict efficiency from the look of a person's office. Efficient people show a thin layer of clutter in a neat and orderly office. Cluttered, disorderly offices are strong clues to inefficient occupants. Neatness pays dividends in time and effectiveness."

• An automobile plant manager: "With the current push for efficiency, I have adopted a new policy about routine meetings. I never start one unless I know what time it should end. This way, there's pressure every minute to get business accomplished quickly. And we do."

• A Midwest attorney: "I log in my billable hours, but no longer with paper and pen. Now I record on a pocket recorder the times when I start or stop work on every item. My assistant then computes the billable time for each client."

• A theatrical producer: "For me, time is money. I have to plan every project and estimate the cost of each phase. At first I lost money on inaccurate estimates. Now, after practice, I can look at a six-month project and plan within a day or two the actual time required."

• An advertising executive: "It took me 15 years to unlearn a bad habit. I always gave my time to anyone who rang the loudest bell. Now I refuse to hear those bells. My time is reserved first for work I want most—the highest priority."

• A manufacturing vice-president: "Last year I started eating lunch regularly with my plant managers. In a month, I heard about three costly situations *before* they got out of hand. Since then, a dozen more. The meetings save time. I used to waste it reading reports that ignored the same problems."

And so it goes in optimizing time. Now, the field trip under your belt, you're ready to dig into the science of priority-propelled time management—ready to dissect the rights and wrongs of the people you've visited. Start with the To–Do List, your cornerstone tool.

PART

GETTING A GRIP ON TIME

CHAPTER 3

THE DAILY TO–DO LIST: YOUR BASIC TOOL

"To choose time is to save time."

—Francis Bacon

Ko-Ko, the "cheap tailor" turned Lord High Executioner in *The Mikado,* was a great organizer. To demonstrate his orderliness in the Mikado, he compiled "a little list" of "society offenders who never would be missed." Thus he could display a victim list when he got called upon to discharge official headsman duties.

Ko-Ko, although new to executions, knew the basic principle of time management: First, you make "a little list." A century later, we still utilize this fundamental tool. It will prevail. Without your To–Do List, you aren't in the game. It's as fundamental in time management as the carefully tailored business plan is in raising corporate capital.

Your To–Do List is the cornerstone of priority-powered time management. Use it effectively and your odds for successful time-walloping are favorable. Try to get by without it and your time management will be a flop. It's that simple.

THE MODERN LITTLE LIST

Although *The Mikado* is still performed around the world, "the little list" branched off as a business tool early in the 20th century when Charles Schwab, Bethlehem Steel president, confronted consultant Ivy Lee with an unusual challenge. And the story goes like this:

"Show me a way to get more things done," he demanded. "If it works, I'll pay you anything within reason."

Lee handed Schwab a piece of paper. "Write down the things you have to do tomorrow." Schwab completed the list. Lee said: "Now number these items in the order of their real importance." Schwab did. Lee said: "The first thing tomorrow morning, start working on number one and stay with it until it's completed. Then take number two, and don't go any further until it's finished or until you've done as much as you can on it. Then go to number three, and so on. If you can't complete everything on schedule, don't worry. At least you will have taken care of the most important things *before* getting distracted by items of less importance.

"The secret is to do this daily. Evaluate the relative importance of the things you have to get done, establish priorities, record your plan of action, and stick to it. Do this every working day. After you've convinced yourself this system has value, have your people try it. Test it as long as you like, and then send me a check for whatever you think the idea is worth."

In a few weeks Schwab mailed Lee a check for $25,000. He later called this the most profitable lesson of his business career.

Thus Ivy Lee and Charles Schwab launched modern time management as a science. Dozens of techniques have been added since. But the To–Do List—with items ranked by importance—remains basic to the process. Like most great ideas, it appears almost simplistic at first glance. Yet it works and will continue to work.

Richard Considine, president of Lincoln Logs Ltd., Chestertown, New York, the housing company, is a great believer in "the little list."

"Each evening I make a list of the ten most important projects to be done," Considine says. "Then next day I make a new list—incorporating what wasn't resolved from the day before. I find priorities change. What was most important today isn't the most important tomorrow. When I find one of our managers getting off the track, I often find he or she isn't working the little list."

"The little list"—as basic as block, tackle, and run in football. Yet how often coaches go back to basics to get the team functioning again! Fundamental rules endure because they've proved out over the years.

HOW TO DO A SUCCESSFUL TO–DO LIST

1. Get in the habit of writing a To–Do List every day.
2. Be realistic and aware of the limitations of your time frame.
3. Don't overschedule.
4. Allow a time cushion.
5. Review your list every morning.
6. Add more items as you do them.
7. Before doing each item, ask, "Why me?" Delegate when possible.
8. Group related activities.

If it's that simple, why doesn't everyone do it? *Simple* doesn't necessarily mean *easy*. As you know from your own experience, it's seductively easy to slip into performing less important work first. Why? *Because the important jobs are often harder*. And you avoid them by hopping on routine chores. You look busy; you are busy. It is real work. It keeps you from wrestling with the tough unfamiliar jobs you feel are going to cause trouble. But, as a consequence, the top-priority task goes begging.

Here are other excuses—many of them—for not doing "the little list." See if they sound familiar:

- *"Takes too much time."* Yet a top sales manager says he *saves* more than 150 hours a year—just by writing weekly schedules and working with them in front of him.
- *"Why write it down? I know what I must do."* Yet the list keeps pulling your attention/energies toward your targets. It helps offset the office distractions.
- *"Too busy."* A respected graphics agency had been losing clients but didn't know why. The company had ex-clients interviewed by a consultant. Response: The agency's work was outstanding—but always late. Investigation showed the agency's managing director was always very busy. But he couldn't manage time. He was always late.

People take cues from the boss. If the boss is indecisive, subordinates will be, too.

When the managing director saw clients departing, he acquired a planner book (now they're used throughout his company) and put himself on daily/weekly schedules. Visits to clients, which he'd neglected, became priorities. He scheduled work, followed the schedules, saved his business. He discovered that when you neglect tackling priority work, you're operating below your potential at best. At worst, you're in trouble.

HOW TO ANALYZE YOUR TO-DO LIST

Your time log is your task inventory. Review each item for:

1. *Necessity*. Scrutinize each task to be sure it is necessary. All too often we continue to do things past usefulness (e.g., monthly reports where information is no longer used).
2. *Appropriateness*. Who should perform the task (i.e., appropriateness to department and/or skill level)? Reassignment of work beneath your skill level helps you and the organization.
3. *Effectiveness*. Is this a task you should be doing now, positioned against your priorities and goals?
4. *Efficiency*. Once satisfied you are doing *necessary*, *appropriate*, and *effective* work, ask: "Is there a better way?" Look for faster methods, better procedures.

WORKING YOUR PLANNER BOOK

You read the words *planner book*. You can get ordinary blank notebooks and draw the format or you can get a printed version called Day-Timers. Homemade or ready-made, your planner/ diary must be:

- *Multipurpose.* Scattered, redundant records are frustrating: Some struggle with an appointment book, a reminder file, a pocket calendar, a wall or desk calendar, a free-floating sheaf of out-of-pocket expenses, and scraps of paper containing bright ideas and notes from conversations. Too much. Use one, multipurpose planner book.
- *Personal.* Nobody can manage your time for you. So use a planner suited to your personal use.
- *Convenient.* Personal often means portable. Some use a pocket-size planner out of office, a desk-size in-house. To really help, your planner must be ready where you are.
- *Orderly.* Many favor a format of each day on two facing pages.

A full page is earmarked to be filled in during the day as tasks are performed. The hour scale down the page allows you to draw brackets showing exact time for each activity. On the facing page is an appointments and scheduled events section—divided into morning, noon, afternoon, night. You check appointments at a glance. A section records travel, entertainment, other expenses. The rest of the page is your *To Be Done Today* space. Here you put a first-things-first plan into practice.

BENDING TIME TO YOUR WILL

You can control time by scheduling skills in your *To Be Done Today* and *Appointments* lists. Many feel: "I don't get enough done—but I don't know why. I just don't know where the day goes!" The answer is in your records. You'll be surprised. Physician, heal thyself! Ask: "Does time mesh with each item's importance?" Then cut or reduce time spent on low-yield activities.

Your planner book is a working tool. Keep it open on the desk. A glance reminds you of phone calls, luncheon dates, meetings, report deadlines. With the book open you just aim your eyes.

In evaluating your list, ask: What's most urgent? Next most? What doesn't relate to goals? What can you put off until tomorrow? What can someone else do? Set priorities based on goal achievement, not ease of doing. As goals and priorities change, change your list. Allocate time blocks for specific tasks. Block time allows you to prepare psychologically. As assigned time draws near, you are equipped to devote enthusiastic attention to each job.

"Fill surprise surplus time," advises Nevada travel agent Mike Cummings. "Even the best planners face unexpected time. Don't waste it. Use this found time for meditation, reflection, or adjustment of your To–Do List; or keep less urgent (but important) tasks to throw in the breach: letter writing, returning telephone calls, conversations with staff, homework for an upcoming sales presentation."

What it boils down to is budgeting your time the way you budget other assets. Decide what goals you want to achieve, then outline steps you take to get there. Focus activities on these goals. After you audit your activities for several days, you'll get a good idea of where time is going. Then you're ready to bend time to your need.

Managing Time Day by Day

For each project, draw up an action plan. Even if you don't follow it entirely, you'll learn much during the planning. Write out your action plan. Do I hear, "It takes too long to write it down!"? Translation: "I don't want to bother thinking before I start." You're implementing the old French cavalry motto: "When in doubt, charge at a full gallop." Colorful? Yes. Disastrous? Often!

Once you have developed your action plan, transfer project dates to your monthly planner. Post starting and milestone dates for each activity. Remember: Certain processes require specific time estimates.

Your To–Do List is a key aid in prioritizing. It's also mentally nourishing to cross items off. Your To–Do List not only helps you remember, it *allows* you to forget. Write it down—then forget it. Don't use brainpower to remember trivia. Plan your day or others will plan it for you. Don't approach each day with a "Take me, I am yours" attitude. Think of commitments (rather than appointments) to yourself and to others.

Play your time planner like an instrument. After you mark off long-range activities and fixed commitments (trade shows, meetings), mark in repetitive meetings (e.g., staff meetings every Monday). Then mark off 8–16 hours of block time per week for yourself.

At the outset, you may not know how you'll use each block. But as important jobs arise, you'll fill in the reserved blocks. Aggressively defend your block time against all interruptions. It's vital.

Mechanics of Time Logging

Brush up on these points before you start each day:

- Every single time you shift your attention, record the new item. Doing it every 15 minutes? You simply miss too much that way!
- Be specific. General language weakens your log. A ten-minute block labeled *phone calls* won't tell at day's end which were necessary and which were time wasters.
- Record *everything*. Don't skip daydreaming, socializing, brief interruptions. You're trying to gauge how much time is frittered away on such minor activities.
- If you log all at once, the temptation to make yourself look good is irresistible. If you record throughout the day, this tendency is less likely. The time log forces you to face reality.

But there's a bonus. Writing things down forces you to be aware of mistakes *while* they're happening. Self-correction is almost automatic.

CHAPTER 4

PLANNING: THE LITTLE PARACHUTE THAT OPENS THE BIG PARACHUTE

**"How pleasant it is, at the end of the day
No follies to have to repent,
But reflect on the past and be able to say
That my time has been properly spent."**

—JANE TAYLOR

To know where you're going, you need to schedule time for *planning*. In scheduling time, allocate yourself a certain amount of quiet time every day to set priorities, put your subconscious to work, think creatively, relax, and/or develop new skills. For some, this is the first thing they do. Others slate a planning time at the start of the day and at day's end.

When you make up a daily schedule, be sure to leave time between appointments to deal with sudden emergencies. Transition time (those short periods of time between major activities) can be reserved for simple 5–15 minute tasks. Utilize the planning system you're most comfortable with. The only alternative not allowed: no planning at all. Then you're a ship without a rudder.

Use Your Prime Energy Time for Priority Tasks

Let's say you always feel great first thing in the morning. Your energy is at its peak from 7:00 A.M. until just before noon. You arrive at the office at 8:45 to review the day's work with your assistant. A voice follows you: "Could you approve these overtime slips and sign the checks?" "Might as well get it over with now," you mutter, vaguely recalling a "do-it-now" principle. "Hang on, Susan."

She hangs on. You sign form after form. She disappears. Other shadows replace her to drop papers on your desk. The telephone rings. More visitors. The intercom buzzes. Morning mail. Your enthusiasm begins to wane and you decide on an early coffee break. Nearly two hours have slipped away. Not only have you not accomplished anything important, but you've squandered the most valuable part of your day—your prime time.

The Quiet Hour

One of the most productive management techniques ever devised is the quiet hour. For one hour a day, no phone calls, no visitors, no chitchat, no "ho-rah"—just quiet, uninterrupted work. Your assistant fields all calls and visitors and takes messages for callbacks. To the world, you're out.

Should there be exceptions? As few as possible.

The benefit? You accomplish in one quiet hour what would normally take three. The best time for the quiet hour? First thing in the morning, before calls and meetings get up to speed. If you are indeed a morning person, schedule your quiet hour during this early period. Close your doors. Have calls and visitors intercepted. Don't schedule appointments or make outgoing calls during this quiet hour. Instead, spend the time and the abundance of energy working on that task that will make the greatest contribution to your organizational goals.

You never allow interruptions when you're in conference. You view it as rude to talk on the telephone, receive visitors, or be inattentive in such situations. You have just as much right (maybe more) to hold private meetings with yourself. In fact, you owe it to yourself to schedule interruption-free time each day to maximize your effectiveness.

You can get twice as much done in an uninterrupted hour. The average executive is interrupted every eight minutes. How can you possibly be effective when you have to stop and reorient yourself every eight minutes?

Early morning may not be best for your quiet period. When you feel wide-awake, refreshed, enthusiastic—that's the time to schedule a meeting with yourself.

Don't waste prime time sorting mail or cleaning out a desk drawer. Invest prime time in important (perhaps difficult) tasks: planning, budgeting, completing a major report or presentation. If your time is worth $100, then the hourly cost of your prime time will be closer to $200. Don't spend $200 to straighten a desk drawer, open mail, or share a coffee with peers. It's more than money. It's your life you're giving away.

If your prime time is 8:30 to 10:00 A.M., block that time out on your calendar. Label it *meeting*. If someone asks, "Can I see you first thing Thursday?" you say, "Well, I have a meeting until 10:00 A.M. How about 10:30?"

You may respond to all of this: "I can't reserve a quiet period on a regular basis. I have to answer the phone. I don't have a private office. The boss keeps interrupting." But you can. If all else fails, spend your quiet hour in another office, in a conference room, or at home.

ESTABLISHING YOUR OWN TIME POLICY

Being effective is planning weeks and months ahead. This requires realistic estimates of how long each task will take. It calls for quiet self-discipline, concentration, and the ability to resist distractions. Above all, it means developing a time policy. A time policy ensures use of your prime time for priority tasks—leaving routine activities for the doldrums.

You've already started a time policy with prime time for priority work. Now extend your time policy to cover your entire day. The habit (as it soon becomes) of performing the same tasks at the same time each day reduces the time it takes to get in gear. It also allows you to use natural breaks (coffee breaks, lunch, quitting time) as deadlines to prevent jobs expanding to fill available time (Parkinson's Law). This is particularly helpful with meetings that take twice as long as they should.

Guard your prime time jealously. If you don't, you'll find yourself scheduling appointments or making calls during the most valuable part of your day. Set meetings late in the afternoon. Meetings end quicker when five o'clock looms. Day's end is also a good time to hand out assignments. Resist the temptation to assign tasks as they occur to you. Make a list during the day and then interrupt your staff only once. During your sluggish hours schedule visitors, return telephone calls, and work on "must-do" items that don't require too much concentration.

Once you've drawn up your own personal time policy, make employees and associates aware of it. Time is the ultimate money. No money can be generated without the time. But remember, you only have a finite amount of time. Invest it wisely. This requires planning.

This one change—first priorities first—will produce immediate benefits:

- You will be doing the most important task when you are at your best, and therefore you can do a better job.
- The rest of the day is downhill.
- When you're working on your top priority it's much easier to resist interruptions (few if any will be as important).
- Even if nothing else in your plan gets done, you leave at day's end having accomplished your top priority.

Make Your Daily Plan

List essential tasks for today. The "musts"—any portion of a major project due today; an assignment from your boss, a critical report. Then rank order them by priority. You're going to tackle number one first. Give yourself a deadline for achieving each. This provides reasons for saying no to interruptions. Deadlines are evidence to yourself and others.

Schedule Appointments

Note meetings, one-on-one conferences, callbacks, appointments, luncheons. Written and spoken words continually shape and change the daily plan. Also note the blocks of time you have set aside for accomplishing specific tasks. Ensure that you work on recurring tasks at the same time each day—the time most productive and convenient for you. Schedule an early meeting with your assistant to go over the day and strategy for accomplishing critical items.

Stick to Your Plan

Put your day's goals and deadlines where they are visible to you all day long. This list is your primary tool for staying on track. If by 9:30 you can see you haven't made much progress toward your 10:00 deadline, you know what to do.

When someone asks for "a few minutes" of your time, look at your daily deadlines and see if you *have* a few minutes to give away. If you like, make the deadline the bad guy. ("My deadline says . . .") If you do not plan your day, other people will "plan" it for you; they will determine *your* priorities.

Planning goals and priority tasks for the day is the most important activity in time management. And to make sure the planning sticks, you must *write it down*. With a written daily plan, you're in control of your time. Without it, your day will be a frustrating rumble of minor crises, interruptions, and dead ends.

EXPERIENCING AN IDEAL DAY

The time planner focuses on the ideal day for the same reason the student of sculpture studies Michelangelo's *David*. Even though you won't attain the ideal day (nor do we expect another Michelangelo), studying the ideal will upgrade your final product.

On your ideal day, you wake up alert, refreshed, in a positive state of mind. After eating a nourishing breakfast, you allow a time cushion for getting to work in case of traffic delays. En route to the office, you listen to music or educational tapes.

At work, your day is already planned. Your personal time log tells you the work you plan to accomplish during the day. By adding and subtracting you've outlined a successful day. Your To–Do List is realistic; you'll add items if you finish early. Your desk is clean from yesterday's day's end cleanup.

You check with staffers: "Any pressing questions?" You meet briefly with your boss and discuss major plans for the day.

TIME LAB
Q&A ON PLANNING

Q. Isn't *planning* just a buzzword for getting organized?

A. No. It's a management system that—if implemented—saves three hours for each hour invested. How's that for return on investment?

Q. Okay if you have computer access. I don't.

A. All you need is paper forms and a pen. List daily goals and deadlines. Rank items by importance, not by ease or preference.

Q. I know you're going to hop on me. But I really don't dare take time to plan!

A. Hop on you? No. Just state the facts. Planning—that three-to-one payoff—deserves time. Take it. Wouldn't you "hop on" any investment that returned three for one?

Q. In my work, we go from crisis to crisis. Who can plan?

A. Most crises stem from lack of long-range planning. You thrive on crisis? Don't believe it. You get by *in spite of* crisis.

Q. I have difficulty assigning priorities. After all, I don't have a crystal ball.

A. Good. Fortune-telling isn't recommended in management. Yes, assigning priorities is difficult. You're allocating your most *precious* commodity—your time—to your *most important* needs. As one manager said: "Guess that's why they pay me the big bucks."

Q. I'm shocked that time management science allows "good enough" on routine jobs. Shouldn't we always strive for excellence?

A. Set priorities. For reasons of physical health and sanity, you can't do everything. Time does run out. Your goal: a project that produces actionable results. Winston Churchill once said, "PERFECTIONISM is spelled PARALYSIS."

Q. I know what to do. Can't I just come in and start doing it?

A. No memory is perfect. Your To–Do List must be in writing to be revised as the day progresses and shifts. Airline pilots don't leave the ground without a written flight plan. They revise that plan as weather and circumstances change. So must the manager. Planning in writing is vital.

You hang out your quiet hour sign. In this hour, you'll accomplish what used to take up to three hours. You start on the most important high-payoff project. Then you work on another major project until your quiet hour is up.

You manage interruptions assertively. You ask people to group questions rather than trail one question at a time. When someone does come in, you inquire how much time is needed and hold to that. If more time is required, you arrange a later appointment.

You've informed callers of the best time to reach you. Your assistant holds all low-priority items until you meet later. Messages go in a special spot. You're free to check the grouped messages as the day goes on.

You group your phone calls and jot down what you want to say beforehand. Your speakerphone allows you to work on other items while you're waiting for answers. An autodialer redials the number if it's busy. If you elect to be put on hold, you have interim work handy.

During break you reflect on the morning. Then you tie up loose ends, check messages, return phone calls, and go to staff appointments to discuss lengthier matters. Before lunch, take ten minutes to straighten up your office.

After a light lunch, you take a short walk and return relaxed. When you open your mail, dump or delegate as much as possible. Put material that isn't time-critical into your briefcase to read later. Only about one-fourth of the mail demands your careful attention. You work on it until your meeting.

At the meeting, you follow your policy of time limits on meetings and advance agendas. Consequently, everyone has thought about the items earlier and the meeting is on target.

Back at your desk, you work to natural stopping places, and to completion. A logical progression throughout the day has kept your energy high. At break time you find a hideaway and meditate. After ten minutes, you return feeling refreshed and clearheaded.

At your afternoon appointment your conferrer is prepared, so no time is wasted. Your second appointment is 15 minutes late so you chip away at your "delay" reading. You scan contents and tear out articles you want to keep. Wham! The rest goes into the deep six.

Before you go home you plan tomorrow's To–Do List. You spend five minutes again straightening up your office. On the way home, you listen to music tapes and congratulate yourself on your productive day.

It's been a great day. You've replaced old, ineffective habits with priority-based strategy. Now you set goals and priorities. Your desk and files are organized. You handle paperwork quickly, deal assertively with interruptions, delegate when possible, and start and finish projects on time. Through priority-powered time management, you are building *real* achievement and a richer life for yourself.

CHAPTER 5

EFFECTIVE, YES! EFFICIENT, NO! KEY TO PRIORITY TIME

"Time is the measure of business, as money is of wares."

—Francis Bacon

Time management values *effectiveness* over efficiency. *Efficiency* refers to how *well* you do something. Effectiveness testing determines whether you should be doing it at all! As Peter Drucker, the eminent management counsel, put it: "Better to do the right *thing* than to do things *right.*"

You have a list of people you must telephone concerning an upcoming meeting. If you think *efficiency*, you consider the best time to call, whether their names might be put on automatic dialing cards, whether the list is accurate and current, and so on. But if you think *effectiveness*, you ask: "Is calling these people the best use of time?" You examine delegating the task or eliminating it altogether, so your time can be used more effectively.

Ask yourself: "Am I focusing on *results* or *activities?*" Focus on activities and at day's end you haven't really accomplished anything. Focus on results. Here's how:

• *Don't get swept up in day-to-day work.* This requires self-discipline. Set specific objectives and pursue them vigorously. Specific objectives are defined as:

- Written
- Measurable
- Expressed in results, not activities
- Realistic, challenging, yet attainable
- Keyed to date of accomplishment

• *Focus first on important* and *urgent tasks.* Too often you'll find yourself pursuing *urgent*—but not important—tasks.

• *Prioritize for effectiveness.* No point doing a job more efficiently if you shouldn't be doing that job at all. Remember the veteran carpenter's advice: "Measure *twice* and cut *once.*"

ANALYZING YOUR TIME LOG

By putting a dollar value on your time, you can use the cost to determine whether achievement is worth the investment. Mark off on paper 15-minute segments for the week. Then identify each of your activities in one of these ways:

- *Long-run value.* Hours invested in meaningful results designed to significantly enhance performance. Example: actual selling time with qualified customer.
- *Essential maintenance.* Required to support long-run goals (travel time, certain paperwork, sales calls on good prospects).
- *Enjoyable.* Items that are simply fun. (Socializing with an established customer who's become a friend.)
- *Other.* Doesn't fall into the first three categories. If in doubt, put it here.

You'll probably find your *Other* category larger than you'd like. Start reallocating your time. Here are ways:

- If you have trouble saying no, take assertiveness training. The time savings can be well worth the investment.
- One hour of uninterrupted time is worth two to three hours of interrupted time. Schedule block time each week. Then break large jobs into small parts. You can eat an elephant—one bite at a time.
- "Management is a series of interruptions, interrupted by interruptions." Attack interruptions that are deferrable or avoidable. Interruptions destroy work flow and hamper productivity.

TIME NUGGETS: WHEN PERFECTIONISM WASTES TIME

Rid yourself of time-consuming perfectionism and add hours of productive time each week.

- ***Eschew perfection.*** **Stop having routine memos and letters retyped because of minor typographical errors. Exception: any important correspondence.**
- ***Dictate letters, memos, and reports only once, then let them fly.*** **Let your assistant draft a reply to correspondence. But first tell the transcriber what you want the letter to say.**
- ***Don't confuse neatness with efficiency.*** **Straightening up is often just an excuse for putting off a job. Organized clutter makes many jobs easier.**
- ***Share your work load with others.*** **You'll be pleased at how most of your co-workers respond.**

THE VALUE OF SETTING PRIORITIES

Learn to say yes to "Are you busy?" and no to "Gotta minute?" If you have an office door, close it. Arrange your desk to avoid eye contact with a potential interrupter. In our society, eye contact makes interruption virtually mandatory. (Eye contact may offer other benefits. Interruptions are not among them.)

Block off the telephone during certain hours. Establish a system for messages. Use voice mail. Program your answering machine to convey time-saving messages. Avoid devices to "improve communications" such as beepers, paging systems, two-way radios. They merely add to the cacophony of modern society. Use the fax machine. It communicates without unnecessary conversation.

When you do allow an interruption, give it your full attention; preoccupation is the enemy of communication. Keep each interruption short and maintain an interrupted attitude. (Yes, you *can* do this and still pay close attention.)

Make Lists

Making lists is the difference between spinning wheels and confidently pursuing objectives. Lists point your direction. Make daily lists of tasks and activities and include meetings, telephone calls, memos, letters, and chores. Your lists should be a blueprint of your long-range and short-term goals, both personal and professional. Goals not clear? Then here's the first item on tomorrow's list; set goals for the week, month, year.

As you complete tasks, cross them off. The sense of accomplishment motivates and energizes. Lists are the first step toward becoming that noted busy person with time to solve problems. ("Want something done? Ask a busy person!")

Set Priorities

Don't allow your daily lists to drive you crazy. There's always one more prospect to see, one more customer task to do. It's open-ended. For the sake of your own health and sanity, remember that you can't do everything. Time does run out.

So review your list. Evaluate. What's most urgent? Next most? What relates and doesn't relate to goals? What can you put off until tomorrow? What can someone else do for you? Set your priorities based on their importance to solving problems and reaching goals, not on which is easier. Then, and only then, have you road-mapped a productive day.

ORGANIZING MECHANICS

Get on top of small, mechanical matters—lest *they* get on top of *you*. Remember the little foxes. They only pilfered a bit each night; but in six months they had enough grapes to start a winery. So it is with thieves of time. Here are ways to thwart them:

- To nail down effectiveness, clear your desk of all unnecessary chaff, including pictures of the family or your prize boa constrictor. Put distractions behind you (the back table is fine). Work on one thing at a time.
- File folders are cheap relative to priceless time. Use folders extensively. Do not fumble with loose papers!
- Start a tickler file—a series of folders numbered 1–31 and another set labeled January through December. A project to be resumed in May goes in May's file. At the beginning of each month, open the month's folder and place each item in the appropriate day's slot. (See Chapter 13.)
- Don't allow junk mail to be dumped into your In-Box. Invest time in communicating how you want mail prioritized. Never use your In-Box as a Hold-Box, or else you'll reshuffle the same papers throughout eternity.
- Above all, don't allow yourself to be diverted by trivial requests. Otherwise people will regard you as a wonderful let-George-do-it person—but unworthy of promotion.
- Develop forms to handle routine tasks. Handle each piece of paper once and only once.
- Always be willing to invest minor money and minor energy to stop daily time wasting. Managers get paid for getting others to perform.
- Beware of Parkinson's Law: "Work expands to fill time." When you don't have much time to accomplish a job, jump in and get it done.

Admittedly, from time to time things come up that are even more important than your quiet hour. These things do preempt your quiet hour. But they shouldn't happen often. When they do, be aware of the cost. You may not be able to place a premium on your prime time. However, do keep it for yourself and it will increase your effectiveness considerably. Priority-powered time management calls for effectiveness first and efficiency second.

Heed Othello's final lament—about successful *efficiency* contrasted with disastrous *effectiveness*: ". . . must you speak of one that loved not wisely but too well."

CHAPTER 6

SAVE PRIORITY TIME BY REDUCING STRESS

"Thus the whirligig of time brings in his revenges."

—SHAKESPEARE

One intense young manager told his analyst about his round-and-round problem: "The *work* causes my stress. Then the *stress* keeps me from doing my work. I'm on a downhill spiral."

"Outline a typical day," the analyst asked. The manager started his oration. After 15 minutes, the analyst held up his hand in protest.

"That's enough! You've just detailed enough to keep you going for two days. You need a system of time management keyed to priorities. The sure knowledge that you're in charge of yourself is the surest way to relieve stress."

"Of course I know about time management," the manager said. "It takes all the fun out of work."

The analyst shook his head. "If forgetting appointments, missing deadlines, and working until midnight is fun, be my guest! But if you find these problems bring on stress—as they do in your case—then you've got to take your time schedule in hand."

Here are other solutions that squelch stress by means of scientific time control:

- *Cancel all meetings.* Ian Donnelly, CEO of Flexmaster, a heating/ventilation/air-conditioning (HVAC) manufacturer in Richmond Hill, Ontario, found that much stress stemmed from regular meetings—getting ready for them, wondering why they don't accomplish anything.

"So I solved the problem by canceling all regular meetings, period," Donnelly said. "The stress factor has been reduced considerably."

Now he holds individual one-on-one encounters—to solve a specific problem or to make a decision. Says Donnelly: "We now have no meeting agendas, no soapboxing, no personal platforming, no general gossip, no discussion of sports scores. What a wonderful way to practically eliminate stress!" This easy solution saves time twice: (1) meetings eliminated, and (2) stress eliminated.

How did Donnelly make this decision? "Every time I'd call a branch office and ask for someone I always heard: 'In a meeting.' When I'd finally get the callback, I'd say, 'What did you accomplish at the meeting?' Since no one could ever report even one achievement, we axed all regular meetings. We're happy, more productive, and it's far less stressful!"

• *Skip half the meetings.* Meetings that leave decisions up in the air breed more (equally useless) meetings. And stress. If you're invited to a useless meeting, ask yourself if you really have to go. Don't feel self-important and go without sufficient thought. Or go to less than half the meetings you're invited to. Make polite excuses: the most believable excuse—"I'm attending another meeting!" If you do go, tell the chairperson how long you're able to stay (rarely longer than an hour). And don't speak up just to let everyone know you're present. If you cannot contribute, keep quiet. At the end of your time—leave. (For more on meetings, see Chapter 8.)

• *Be physically active to relieve tension.* Ed Laufer, a Bear Stearns broker, found that his job lived up to its reputation for pressure. Friends recommended daily exercise to allow sore muscles to replace a battered psyche. But Laufer, a romantic soul, found gym workouts dull and demeaning.

"Now, *if* exercise were as interesting as ballroom dancing, I'd be all for it," he said. "That's it!" his friend said. "Take ballroom dancing twice a week."

Now, eight hours each week, Laufer jumps into patent leather pumps and skips off to dance class. His form may never equal Fred Astaire's, but his tension is reduced. His stress level has dropped, and his productivity's up. For Laufer, investing in exercise that's fun proved to be priority-activated time control.

What kind of exercise is fun for you?

• *Work faster and feel better.* Reduced stress is a bonus you get with effective time management. There are not enough hours in the day to deal with the people you must see, the meetings you must attend, the papers you must process. Rarely enough hours for returning phone calls, much less for thought and reflection. How do you make more hours? Do everything faster and don't waste time! Don't say, "Too simplistic!" until you read on. It can be done!

• *Leave the work at the office.* Occasionally you may feel you need to take work home. If you find yourself doing it on a regular basis, something's wrong. Except in an emergency, working at home is counterproductive; it drains your energies, and it may alienate your living companion. It can also dampen your drive to get things done at the office. ("If I don't get this finished today, there's always tonight.") Yes, a long document or a complicated report may sometimes require it, but don't overdo—lest you become a dull dog and a bore to the people you live with.

• *Make quick decisions.* Whether you make them quickly or slowly, many of your decisions will be wrong. You might as well make them all quickly. Above all, quick decisions save much stress.

• *Save time in a crisis.* A crisis is a dangerous, unpredictable, or fluid stress situation. You must act swiftly (with little or no time for reflection) to prevent harm (or to gain credit). The most important rule: Stay at your post. Resist the temptation to leave your desk and do all the fire fighting yourself. The second most important rule: Give clear instructions—in person, by phone, or by fax. Giving orders is a science that's learnable. Briefly explain the situation. State what you want to achieve. Describe the method of achieving it. Finally, arrange for frequent reports from your people.

• *Manage the boss.* Handling your boss is a formula for either stress or harmony—depending on how well you do it. Put it down as gospel—people skills are your greatest aid in climbing the corporate ladder. Then, as topic A under that, note this: Nowhere is this truer than in communicating with your boss. If your boss doesn't believe you're doing a good

(Text continues on page 47.)

TIME LAB
YOUR SUBCONSCIOUS FEELINGS ABOUT TIME

1. Work on this undisturbed for ten minutes.

2. To the side of each word draw an *abstract* symbol that describes your immediate feelings about the word. Use lines, circles, spirals, and the like. Do not use standard symbols—a happy face for *enjoy,* a clock for *time,* or a star for *perfect.* We need your personal graphic reactions.

3. If you hesitate on a word make a check next to the word. Take a final moment to think of a symbol. If no ideas come, move on.

1. Supervisor	11. Barriers
2. Job	12. Organized
3. Time	13. Me
4. Due dates	14. Agreement
5. Assertive	15. Enjoy
6. Distraction	16. To put off
7. Paperwork	17. Hate
8. Trivia	18. Decisions
9. Telephone	19. Delegate
10. Job site	20. Ideal

HOW TO SCORE AND INTERPRET YOUR TEST

An example of a completed test is shown below. Note graphics in the first column are connected by identifying lines to words with similar graphics in column two. Make similar connecting lines on your test.

To be interpreted: no right or wrong, of course. Test shows how you connect time-oriented thoughts—e.g., a line between *supervisor* and *hate* could mean you (1) dislike your current boss, (2) dislike the supervisory function for yourself, (3) dislike all supervisors on principle, (4) believe your boss hates you. Knowing yourself and your situation makes you uniquely qualified to read your connections.

Possible interpretations of check marks: (1) You are unfamiliar with the connotation or do not feel strongly about it; (2) you have conflicting feelings about the word, preventing a quick decisive graphic rendering; (3) your difficulty is in making decisions—particularly if you checked four or more words.

Your testing results alert you to hitherto hidden feelings about time, thus making you more effective in managing time.

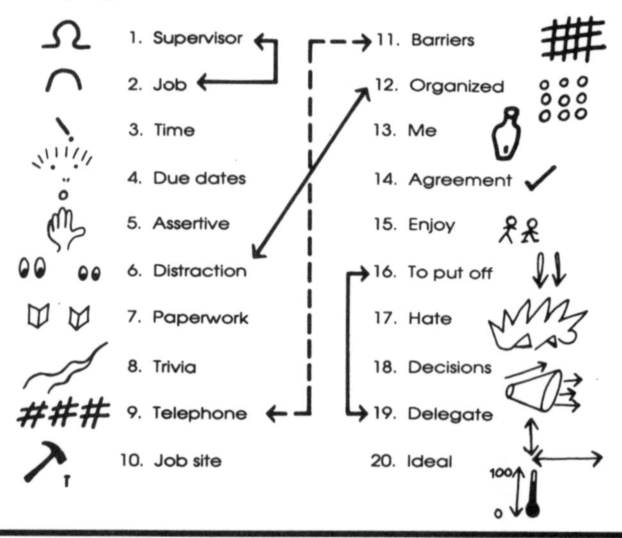

job, it doesn't matter too much what anyone else thinks—you're in the soup. Begin by understanding bosses. Bosses have an ego all their own. Keep them informed. Become less dependent on their approval. Tell your boss: *"Unless I hear otherwise,* I'll go ahead and order supplies early." If your approver is too busy to get back to you, you have his or her implied consent to go ahead in your own time-effective way.

• *Carefully mix work and breaks.* To work for long periods without taking a break is not an effective use of time. Energy decreases, boredom sets in, and physical stress and tension accumulate. Irritability, chronic fatigue, headache, anxiety, and apathy all stem from lack of variety. For a change of pace, switch from a mental to a physical task. Move from a sitting to a standing position. Walk around the block. A break not only increases efficiency, it relieves tension. Anything that contributes to good health is smart time management.

• *Exercise and eat smart.* If you're too busy to exercise, you're really too busy. Nothing has higher priority than health. If you find time for television, but not tennis or jogging, you're violating the basic rule of time management: Do the most important things first. Your vigor throughout the day is closely related to your physical shape. Good physical condition increases your number of prime-time hours. Eat a substantial breakfast, a light lunch, and an even lighter dinner. Avoid fried foods, sugar, and excessive amounts of caffeine. Exercise regularly, even if it's just walking (really one of the best choices you can make).

• *Take a nap.* The 24-hour day is an accident of astronomy. Most other animals have sense enough to take a nap whenever they need it, day or night. Einstein made a nap part of his daily routine. So did Edison and Churchill. And Presidents Kennedy, Johnson, and Reagan. Could your work cycle involve a mid-day nap? It might be worth some arranging. Going flat out all day is hard not only on the body, but on the mind as well. Rid yourself of accumulated tension and you'll be further ahead by day's end.

• *Relax.* Relaxation plays a vital role in productivity. Working for long periods without breaks results in decreased energy, physical stress, and tension. After work hours, restore yourself in order to use time productively tomorrow. Relax with a book unrelated to work. Exercise to keep healthy. Take a lesson from farmers. They know that for soil to produce Grade-A crops, it must occasionally lie fallow. So it is with people, too. "Show me an executive who works ceaselessly at high speed and I'll show you an executive who's high *on* speed," one career woman said. In creative work, you can take out only as much as you put in. Reading, for a manager, *is* stoking the furnace: never mind that while the furnace is being stoked you're lying on the couch.

• *Revitalize your workday*. When work is unrelenting, tension follows. A simple change in attitude can revitalize you:

- Think of work as a game. Enjoy it. When the day's game is over, put it to bed. In the morning, start fresh.

TIME NUGGETS: TIPS ON HANDLING STRESS

- **Work smarter, not harder. Does this activity need doing at all? If so, who should be doing it?**
- **Carry reading material with you. When forced to wait, put your time to use. You reduce stress and gain productivity.**
- **Inevitably, some of your time will be spent on activities outside your control. Accept it.**
- **Don't waste your time feeling guilty about what you don't get done.**
- **Record daily activities, achievements, goals, sources of delay, and time waste. Your notes will reveal all kinds of hidden opportunities.**
- **List items on a 5-minutes-or-less sheet. When you have a few minutes, pick an item from your short-task list.**
- **Continually ask yourself, "What is the best use of my time right now?"**
- **Eat a light lunch. Reward: You don't get sleepy in the afternoon.**

- Maintain psychological distance from the game. You and your work are close, but not Siamese twins.
- Cultivate a confidant to share your triumphs and to console you during setbacks. A friendly ear is a catharsis.
- If your work (no matter how important) is not fun, figure out how to eliminate most of the tedious elements. The CEO of a research firm hated selling but loved unraveling the statistics. He hired a salesperson. Although it strained his resources at first, he did better work. And the salesperson had more to sell. It worked. As a last-ditch move, you may need to find another job that *is* fun.

There is nothing noble about suffering. Many benefits accrue from play and fun. If you do not enjoy a large part of your job, change the job—internally or externally.

• *Manage by objectives.* Knowing where you're going gives you a sense of purpose about the day. But here's the trap: Starting new projects is often more exciting than finishing old ones. The problem: Too many projects-in-work scatters your thinking, undermines your progress, and drags down your energy. Revel in a feeling of accomplishment when you keep putting completed tasks into a large imaginary pipeline.

A final word. Make lulls work for you. Plan to do your trivial work when your energy is low. This way, you still move ahead and are not making excessive demands on yourself.

CHAPTER 7

HOW TO AVOID SELF-INFLICTED DELAY

"One of these days is none of these days!"

—Old English Proverb

Be realistic. Many time-eaters are *not* under your control:

- A command attendance at your boss's daughter's graduation
- Your best customer's expressed desire to see a Broadway show
- A surprise audit appointment with the IRS

Better heed all three. The greater good is at stake.

Do command performances play hob with your time management plans? Yes. But viewed in the context of priority-activated decisions, each qualifies superbly. (To test: Ask yourself, "What will happen if I *don't?*" You'll get a fast answer.)

So your overall priority sense bids you heed some surprises from outside. On the other hand, *other* time wasters are *self-inflicted.* Anytime you cause your own delay you are trashing your own time and need to look for solutions.

Solutions for self-flagellation *do* exist. Take the problems in turn.

Delaying Decisions

The effective manager welcomes decision making: the basic stuff, the protoplasm, of management. Decisions are what you're paid to make. In each case, try to get as many facts as possible because you'll never get them all. When you get all you can, make the decision. Once you make it, assume it's right—even though occasionally you may be wrong.

Don't play it safe. IBM founder Thomas J. Watson said it best: "Each of us must be alert to the dangers of playing it safe. Act courageously on what you believe is right." Hiding behind a committee often produces self-inflicted delay (SID). Eight people get together to rebuild the building. When it doesn't work, you can't put your finger on who made the original decision. Weak executives skulk behind committee skirts.

In establishing your reputation as an effective time manager, you're far better off going out of your way to record as many clear-cut decisions as possible. Ask for responsibility *and* authority. And give your people the same. Tell your staff what you expect and give them the authority to do it. The act of delegation is in itself often a decision subject to SID. On the other hand, don't be a phony delegator—giving work to subordinates just to keep them busy. That's a waste of time *and* effort. Once you give a person a job, step back. Sure, he or she won't do it exactly the way you would have. But judge only by the end result, not the way it was reached.

Don't brood over the possible consequences of a decision. Imagine the worst possible effect of your decision. If you take this thinking to absurd lengths, your fears will move into proper perspective. And don't negate your gut reactions. They could be telling you something. (Educators tell us that students who change the first multiple-choice answer were often right the first time!)

Don't postpone. If you can't make up your mind, set a date for resolution. By removing the immediate pressure, you'll be able to evaluate the options more objectively. Broaden your array of choices. Example: You can't decide whether to hold a sales-incentive trip in Alaska or the Yucatán. Consider other spots and their costs. Then you will have a better idea of how much the Alaskan trip means to you, and you will be able to make a decision that pleases you. Remember, there is seldom an absolute right choice. You simply make up your mind to do something, and then accept the responsibility for it.

Failing to Handle Distractions

Yes, most distractions do come from others. But unless you combat them, they also qualify as self-inflicted. Use these remedies to ward off SID:

- When you are handed another person's work, hand it back—tactfully but firmly.
- Don't spend more time than necessary entertaining visitors. Don't siphon time from your schedule to visit people unexpectedly.
- If you must leave your office, give yourself a time limit and stick to it.
- Burnout from too long on the same channel? Mix the *routine* with the *creative,* the *passive* with the *active.*
- Make better use of other people's work/your own past work in tackling present assignments.
- Arrange travel in straight lines and group your appointments carefully.

Leaving Tasks Unfinished

"Many managers can take a problem apart," one executive recruiter said. "When we're casting for a particularly demanding executive post, we seek the man or woman who can do that and then *put* all the *parts together* in *working* order."

The headhunter was saying: "I am looking for a *closer,* a finisher, a completer." Clearly the top performer is also an excellent priority-activated time manager. The reason? Starting and stopping a project squanders time. Finishing it ("with the parts in working order") saves time and meets company objectives. When you allow interruptions/distractions, you're automatically abandoning your current task. Ditto when you interrupt yourself—daydreaming, taking an unneeded break, leaving one thing to take up another.

Dr. John Mee, former management professor at the University of Indiana's School of Business, says finishers stick with one project until it is completed—occasionally against all odds. Finishers do not tolerate interruptions, except for emergencies. Even then, they resist leaving the current task unless it's clear that (1) the crisis priority is higher than the task at hand, and (2) their assistance is crucial to the crisis.

What drives unfinishers? Why the trail of partially completed

TIME LAB
SIDS THAT OCCUR FROM CAN'T-SAY-NOS

Check those that apply to you:

☐ *Fear of offending*	Develop State Department techniques of saying no. Examples: "Thanks for the compliment, but I'll have to decline." "Sorry, I can't, but let me offer a suggestion . . ."
☐ *No time to think of answer*	Say: "I'll get back to that in a minute." Give yourself time. Delay response.
☐ *Your capabilities are in demand*	Thus saying no is even more imperative. Refuse to spread yourself too thin. Concentrate on your priorities.
☐ *No good excuses*	Sometimes no excuse is better than a lame excuse. Best reason: your own priorities. Keep them visible in your mind. Articulate them to others.
☐ *Lack objectives and priorities*	Danger! Others will determine your priorities.
☐ *Assumption by others that you'll say yes*	You encouraged this assumption by never saying nay. Learn to say no, particularly to inappropriate or thoughtless requests.
☐ *Can't say no to boss*	You can say no by showing your list of agreed-upon priorities. If boss insists, ask for agreement on revised priorities.

projects? They subconsciously fear the work will not be good enough; and they are unable to weigh conflicting priorities.

There are—alas!—compelling reasons for leaving a job in midstream. To overcome: When interrupted in the middle of a task, make every effort to postpone or suggest alternatives. In some cases, leave the task in someone's hands to keep it alive during the interruption. Your plan: to pick up again as soon as humanly possible.

Can't Say No

Many who can't say no are, at bottom, trying to win approval and acceptance. "This is the supreme irony," says James M. Triggs, a firearms industry graphics manager. "By not saying no often enough, they fail to get priority work done. Hence they lose the very approval so eagerly sought."

Unreasoning Fear of Deadlines

As you rise in management, you'll be setting deadlines for your people, and meeting deadlines in your own work as well. Word soon gets around whether a person meets due dates or not. (If you don't, you're putting big rocks in your backpack going up the slope.) Deadline beaters are not time eaters.

If you've ever worked on a newspaper (campus or otherwise) you probably came away with a healthy respect for deadlines. Deadlines occur constantly, and everyone works by the same clock. Produce or perish.

Delay is stultifying. A work session harvests great ideas. Everyone goes away excited. But follow-through is postponed for a few days. Other problems intervene. Then, when people get down to implementation, enthusiasm has wilted, memories have blurred, the thrust is dulled.

People who live by tough deadlines get a lot more done. Some of the best work comes from moving quickly from the heat of ideation to the immediacy of execution. When time is merciless, and people go from the warmth of inspiration right into

TIME LAB
TEST YOURSELF FOR PURE AND SIMPLE PROCRASTINATION

Many who quote Edward Young's "Procrastination is the thief of time" think of procrastination as being synonymous with *delay.* Not so. There are many kinds of delay. However, the P—word means "putting off or failing to take action *without justification.*" In short, pure, undiluted procrastination, if habitual, becomes self-inflicted delay.

Identify the P—word in your life:

☐ *Lack of self-discipline*	Try (1) setting deadlines on tasks, (2) reporting ("going public") those deadlines to others, (3) asking for help in monitoring, (4) submitting regular progress reports (even if not requested), (5) using reminders—lists, an egg timer, a wrist alarm.
☐ *Saying: "I work better under pressure"*	Nobody works better under pressure. A *good* performer under pressure is often *excellent* with proper deadlines.
☐ *Lack of deadlines*	See deadlines as valuable tools (sense of urgency, means of measuring progress). Establish a deadline on each major task.
☐ *Lack of regular monitoring of progress*	This encourages leaving whole jobs until the last minute, practically guaranteeing a crisis. Fast feedback on progress (1) provides motivation to continue and (2) alerts you if you fall behind.
☐ *Doing the easy or trivial first, postponing the difficult*	Under this system, you will almost always ignore effectiveness in your zeal to be efficient. Do number one in importance first! Then number two, and so on.

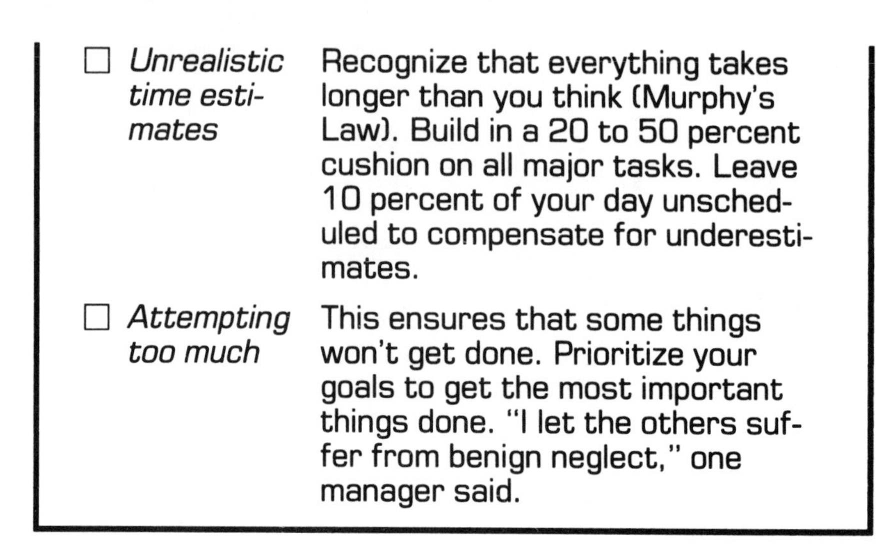

☐ *Unrealistic time estimates*	Recognize that everything takes longer than you think (Murphy's Law). Build in a 20 to 50 percent cushion on all major tasks. Leave 10 percent of your day unscheduled to compensate for underestimates.
☐ *Attempting too much*	This ensures that some things won't get done. Prioritize your goals to get the most important things done. "I let the others suffer from benign neglect," one manager said.

execution, the excitement can be seen shining through the finished product.

Nothing much is accomplished by delay. Remember the old folk axiom: "On the plains of hesitation bleach the bones of countless thousands who, on the threshold of victory, hesitated and, while hesitating, died."

PART

MANAGING TIME WASTERS

CHAPTER 8

THE MEETING: OPPORTUNITY OR TIME WASTER?

"Dost thou love life? Then do not squander time, for that is the stuff life is made of."

—Ben Franklin

A Wisconsin manufacturing company scheduled meetings to discuss ways to improve productivity. After leaving yet another time-consuming session, one employee said: "And we'll *keep* these meetings going until someone figures out why *nothing* is *getting done* around here!"

Does this story reflect real life? All too often! Why?

Meetings are the most firmly entrenched institutionalized time wasters in U.S. business society. No accurate figures exist on hours frittered away in needless meetings. Just as well! If such a count could be verified, the shock to the mass psyche would be lasting—perhaps fatal.

We do know the hour-carnage is horrific. Since we don't have a cure for the meeting, at least we can learn intelligent ways to treat its symptoms.

Why do we (anyone) schedule a meeting? Ironically enough, it's all based on the meeting caller's desire for efficiency and effectiveness in communication and persuasion! He or she strives to get 5, 25, 50, or 105 people in one spot to tell them all (1) how wonderful a development is, (2) how great a customer need is, and (3) how they must stop doing X and start doing Y—or any one of a hundred other variations.

Right away you see the logical division of meetings:

- *Type A meetings*. Those events *you* produce—to sell; persuade; inform an audience about a policy, need, or

technology dear to your heart. (You also see why meetings are so sacrosanct. It makes a difference when it's *your* meeting.)
- *Type B meetings.* Someone else produces an event designed to do ditto about ditto, and you're earmarked as one of the persuadees.

Yes, there is another kind of a meeting, where department heads thrust and parry about ideas for the coming selling season. They get input from production, marketing, legal, personnel. That's really a committee, another great time waster.

But, at bottom, one person is usually convincing other people of the validity (workability, creativity, unquestioned need) of a viewpoint. If you're that person, your meeting is Type A. If you're an attendee, it's a Type B. So, a time waster for some can be a wonderful opportunity for others.

Let's view Type A and Type B meetings separately to see how to treat their symptoms.

TYPE A: MEETINGS YOU CONTROL

Nine times out of ten the Type A meeting, the one you produce and manage, will be in the presentation format. You've attended too many poor presentations. But now you're about to produce an excellent event—your own. To do so, work diligently on *preparation* as well as *execution*.

Preparation

Before you start planning a formal structure (no longer than one hour), ask yourself these questions:

- What are my objectives?

____

____

____

____

- Who is my audience?

____

____

____

____

- What important factors are to be conveyed?

____

____

____

____

- How can I best get them across to this group?

____

____

____

____

- What visual aids will I need?

____

____

____

____

- Where will the presentation be? Any time limitations?

____

____

____

____

Study pertinent background information and data. Employ only the most relevant facts in your presentation. Just as it's essential to know your audience, you also need a thorough professional knowledge of the industry you're approaching—its products, programs, and services.

As you prepare, think graphically. Will a chart, line drawing, or cartoon help? At the presentation site, are walls free of clutter and light enough to use a screen? Are electric plugs accessible?

When you feel your presentation is ready, review the material. Rehearse; correct weaknesses; rehearse more. Remember, only the amateur wings it. The professional knows rehearsal is standard.

TYPE B: MEETINGS YOU DON'T CONTROL

For meetings you don't control, your best bet is: Don't go. Not only will this save valuable time, it will enhance your reputation.

Too much out-time marks you as a meetings junkie—not a serious contender. MJs spend half their time going to meetings, conferences, briefings, conventions, and miscellaneous gatherings of the clan. Between times, they drop names, relay misinterpretations of what a speaker said, and handle trivia that keeps them away from everyday problem solving. MJs are often pleasant, well-mannered, and moderately interesting people. They are experts on the Waldorf, Drake, Fairmont, Century Plaza, and Shamrock-Hilton. They know the best menu choices at the Greenbrier, Homestead, Breakers, and Broadmoor.

The trouble is: MJs toil not, neither do they manage time. Neither do they advance up the ladder.

Okay. You're not an MJ. And you've winnowed down to the meetings you want to (or must) attend. There are still ways to conserve time:

- *Go for just the part that relates to you.* By skipping parts you'll spend more time on priorities your boss expects by tomorrow morning.
- *Use your boss as an excuse.* If another department asks you to "drop by" the committee meeting tomorrow afternoon, get

more information while you build a basis for declining: "There may be a conflict with my boss so I better clear it with him first."

• *Decide things without a meeting.* If someone calls and asks to get together, ask, "Can't we just do it now on the phone?" Or, if a meeting-happy person stops you in the hall, say, "Well, here we are together right now. Why don't we just decide?"

• *Send a written statement instead.* Another manager asks you to attend a meeting but you believe your marginal participation will interfere with priority projects. Call the meeting planner's assistant to ask what's expected. He'll probably say: "She wants you to discuss A and B." Tell him of the conflict with your boss's priorities. Offer to send a written statement on the topics instead. Then, do just that.

• *Take control if the chair is late.* Not only does a tardy chairperson waste precious minutes, it sets a lazy meandering tone for the meeting. Don't wait. Say: "Donna is probably tied up. Why don't we get started? When she gets here, we'll fill her in. This first item, now—what do we all think of it?"

Then, when Donna arrives, summarize: "We discussed the trade show. We took a vote, and it's ten to two against it, if that helps you." Then sit down. You've saved time and made a good point.

• *Take control if the chair arrives but doesn't start right away.* Say loudly and with surprise: "Hey, it's two o'clock." Everyone will check their watches. The chair, chatting with someone up front, will say: "Okay, let's get started here." Everyone will silently say: "Amen to that."

If all else fails, and you're in a dud meeting, it's a good time to make up or edit your To–Do List. This way, priority-activated time management goes on.

Effective Type A and Type B meetings require time and effort. We've all seen too many of the other kind. By putting on excellent events and avoiding Type B meetings when you can, you'll achieve your goals and do your bit for stamping out pointless and senseless meetings. You'll be using your time effectively, and you'll help others go home feeling *they* utilized *their* time wisely!

CHAPTER 9

STARVING OUT THE TIME GOBBLERS

"What a folly to dread the thought of throwing away life at once, and yet to have no regard to throwing away by parcels . . ."

—John Howe

George Smithers, a rising manager, asked his boss about his biggest time management problem—his staff. "I can do *my* work—or could," said Smithers. "But I'm constantly interrupted by the people who *work* for *me*. If I'm stopped every five minutes, I can't do my own work."

This problem bothers many. Don't let it be a serious roadblock to you. Your work and their work can (must!) co-exist.

Sure, an open-door policy is good. But that shouldn't preclude block time when your door is closed—from 9:00 to 11:00 A.M. each Wednesday and Friday, for instance. People will work around that—just as if you were out. (Top managers keep coming back to *block time* again and again as their cornerstone to getting things done.)

So make your open-door policy figurative, not literal, until you get elevated enough to sit around all day, inviting interruptions. (And if this ever materializes, it'll sound suspiciously as though you're on a plateau—because top people don't do it.)

Doors are meant to be closed when you're planning or writing reports. "There is this crazy idea abroad in business today that you only shut your door when you are firing someone," says Bill Marsteller, the ad agency chairman. "Anybody who has invention as a part of his job description is entitled to periods of isolation."

Scotching Drop-In Trade

Your own staff people are not your only visitors.

"Everyone in the company came by this morning," a young manager told her friend at lunch. "What could I do?" (Portrait of an otherwise savvy department head yet to develop her instinct for starving out time gobblers.) Her friend, wiser, said: "Mary, make a distinction between business and social availability. Sure, you're available on business matters—by appointment. You're not available for drop-in socializers."

Then her friend added, only half-kidding: "Put up a sign that says: 'If you have nothing to do, don't do it here.' "

Check off other reasons you get drop-ins (and read what to do about them):

☐ *Open-door policy*	*Open door* does not mean physically open, but open to those who need assistance. Modify your open door by closing it regularly for periods of concentration. Redefine *open* to mean "accessible."
☐ *Inability to terminate visits*	Go to offices of others. Meet them outside your office. Stand up upon entry and keep standing. Preset time limits on visits. Telegraph end ("Is there anything else before I leave?"). Prearrange for assistant to interrupt on "an urgent matter." Or tell it like it is. ("Sorry, gotta get back to other matters now!") Stand up and walk to the door.
☐ *Poor physical location*	Change if possible; if not, avoid eye contact. Find a hideaway to escape to for your quiet hour.

Dialogues That Disperse

Some visitors are persistent, all right. When more drastic action's needed, try these:

• *Set a time limit at the outset.* "Sure, I can help you with that. But I must leave at 10:15. Think we can finish in 15 minutes?" Set your watch alarm. When it rings, get up.

• *Go to the other person's office.* Then you can leave whenever *you're* ready. When someone drops in, get a fix on the problem, then say, "I need ten minutes to wrap up this report. Why don't I come to your office then?"

• *Stand up.* Effective for keeping visits short. Stand up to greet visitors. Find out the need. If it's quick, answer it, or reschedule if needed—all while standing. Once you invite your visitor to be seated, you're in the soup.

• *Find and use a hideaway.* Find an unused conference room, an empty office, a room at the library, the cafeteria at nonmealtimes. Here no one can find you, so interruptions are zero. Work out an agreement whenever someone is out for the day; a needy soul can always use vacant desks for concentrated work.

• *Cut yourself short.* When you see the visitor is going to take a while, say: "Michael, I thought this was going to be a short question, but I see now that it's more than that. I should have asked you how long this was going to take. I have this 10:00 deadline on material for my boss. Can we reset this for tomorrow? Frankly, I don't think I could keep my mind on it right now."

Minimize Interruptions

Since you're going to permit—alas!—some interruptions (if only a *small* percentage of what you once tolerated), here are ways to minimize them:

- Allow a stated time—and only that time—each day for interruptions and unscheduled events. Never allow long-winded visitors to get seated.
- Hold stand-up conferences. Meet visitors outside your office.
- Encourage appointments rather than unscheduled visits.
- Rearrange your furniture so you're not facing the door.
- Remove extra chairs from your office. Close your door.
- Do not contribute unnecessary conversation.
- Avoid people who constantly take advantage.
- When someone asks: "Got a minute?" say no.

Formalize Your Work Methods

Key everything to priorities in time. When reading documents and reports, try to get the gist quickly (not the same as *reading* quickly). Understand the principal arguments rather than read it all. How do you learn to do this? Practice. Moreover:

- Express views concisely, with telegraphic brevity. Practice by shortening every draft to less than half its length. Write by hand or type. Don't dictate.
- Don't rely on the telephone for routine communication. A hand-written note is often faster.
- Conduct meetings effectively and courteously. But force everyone to stick to the point—all the time.
- Make a list of daily priorities and stick to them. But be brave enough to change your timetable to meet changing situations.
- Don't let trivia clutter your day.

Be rough with people who don't appear at the stated hour. If they are not punctual, they evidently have something more important to do. Start without them. Do not mess up the rest of your day because of their sloppiness.

Force people to come to the point. After their explanation and recommendations, your hope is to say yes or no or to give clear direction. If you can't, say: "I'll think about it" and move on to the next item or appointment. Don't waste time going over an issue again and again.

In a complicated discussion, nothing is more time wasting than allowing *background*—which you should have had in advance. Don't hold the discussion until you've been briefed in writing.

Find a polite way of cutting off people who ramble. Make them stick to the point. The best way: Ask clear, precise questions. Insist that they be answered.

Let your staff see you're in a hurry. But never let them think you're harassed—another state entirely. In holding a job-related heart-to-heart, appear to possess all the time in the world. Be gentle and relaxed. Let your assistant blow the whistle when time is up.

Try seeing employees the moment they call, if they want to discuss an important matter. Your answer should be (1) "Come now," (2) "Come in 15 minutes," (3) "Come at 6:15 this evening." You can (must!) always find an extra few minutes for key people.

Forcing the caller to come earlier than expected will significantly reduce the length of the interview. And your willingness to make time instantly enhances your caller's ego.

Writing a note is quicker than talking to people, and usually faster than trying to reach them by phone.

Finally, what about the person (not on your team) who's holding up the approval you need to get your work done on time? Nothing to do, you say? Use the "unless-I-hear" memo. Say: "Attached is a copy of my request for your decision on Project X. It is time for me to take action. *Unless I hear* to the contrary by Friday, August 12, I'll assume that you approve of my outline and will proceed accordingly."

CHAPTER 10

DELEGATION: GIVING IT TO GEORGE AND GEORGINA TO DO

"To be good is noble, but to teach others how to be good is nobler— and much less trouble."

—Mark Twain

Subordinates are clever. If you don't watch out, they'll delegate *their* work to *you*. They do it, say consultants William Oncken, Jr., and Donald L. Wass, so deftly you stagger away without knowing what hit you.

This upward delegation is double-murder to time managers because (1) it keeps them from assigning work that should be delegated, and (2) they walk away with the *added* burden of their employee's work.

Here's how it happens. You walk down the hall and meet subordinate Jack Steiner. "Good morning," Steiner says. "By the way, we've got a problem. You see . . ."

He explains it. You know (1) enough about the project to get worried, but (2) not enough to make an on-the-spot decision. So you say: "Glad you brought this up. I'm in a rush right now. Let me think about it and I'll let you know."

Before you two met, the monkey was on *Jack's* back. After you parted, it was on *your* back. Subordinate-imposed time begins the moment a monkey successfully leaps from the subordinate's back to yours. It does not end until the monkey is returned for care and feeding to its proper owner.

In accepting the monkey, you voluntarily assumed a position subordinate to your subordinate. Why? Because you did two things subordinates do for their boss—(1) accept an assignment, and (2) promise a progress report. Jack (to make sure you don't miss this point) will soon stick his head in the door and cheerily ask, "How's it coming?" ("supervision").

How does it happen? Because the manager and the subordinate assume at the outset that the matter is a joint problem. The monkey then gets astride both backs. All it has to do is move the wrong leg, and the subordinate disappears! To solve this problem, Oncken and Wass say, you should call your subordinate in. Place the monkey on the desk between you and decide jointly what move the subordinate might make next. Once this is decided, the subordinate takes the monkey and leaves.

Even if you cannot decide today, the subordinate takes the monkey with him. He is no longer waiting for the boss to do something. You're waiting for *him* to report action. Explain to Jack: "At no time while I am helping you with a problem will *your* problem become *my* problem. The instant your problem becomes mine, you will no longer have a problem. You may ask my help at any appointed time, and we will make a joint determination of the next move. I will not make any move alone."

Thus you keep the initiative where it belongs—with the subordinate. (Not only will this preserve your time, it's also good management.)

Your job is to develop initiative in subordinates. Once you take it back, your employees will no longer have it and you can kiss discretionary time good-bye. It will all become subordinate-imposed time.

Final advice:

- Feed monkeys by appointment only.
- Feed them face-to-face or by telephone, never by memo. (If by memo, the next move will be yours.)
- Assign every monkey a "next feeding time."

So keep the monkey off your back and you'll gain time to do your own work and provide better supervision. Avoiding *upward* delegations is priority-activated time management at its best. Now let's get on with *downward* delegation.

WHAT (AND WHY) IS DELEGATION?

Management is getting work done through others. Delegating is authorizing others to carry out specific tasks under your general supervision. It frees you to be more productive and creative. It forces you to be more organized because you must outline projects, assign responsibilities, set deadlines, check progress.

Delegating never absolves you of responsibility. You're still accountable. But as you go along, you can train subordinates to carry out more and more to free up greater chunks of your valuable time.

In spite of all the benefits in delegating, many people still resist it. "If I want something done right, I have to do it myself!" they say. Some fear to impose on subordinates. Others are afraid employees will perform too well and maybe take over the assigner's job! Still other managers think they're too busy to train staff.

Always be on the lookout for challenging jobs to delegate. Advance your career by looking not *up* the ladder, but *down* the ladder. Allow others to develop and don't hog the credit. Give subordinates a sense of their importance.

Be quick to praise, be slow to criticize, and, by all means, be (and appear) fascinated by the results. Proper appreciation assures you of cooperation the next time.

The sheer multiplicity of management responsibilities requires delegation. Sure, it involves risks. In giving authority, you lose some control. But you cannot do everything yourself.

DELEGATION IS GOOD—BUT . . .

No management practice is praised more in theory and applied less in practice than delegation. Managers praise it to the skies—for others. "Oh, yes. But in my case . . ."

All right. Put seven popular "yes-buts" under the laser ray of truth:

1. *"I could do it better."* Delegate it anyway. If someone on your team does an outstanding job, your reputation is enhanced. And while you could perhaps do the task better, you cannot do your entire staff's work—no one can.
2. *Anxiety about mistakes.* "I'll have to pick up the pieces." Project an atmosphere where mistakes are tolerated. No pain, no gain. Little of value is accomplished when nothing is risked.
3. *"I'm not comfortable delegating."* It's tempting to retreat to routine tasks you already know how to do—even when those tasks should be delegated to promote growth. As a successful manager, you must move away from work you know and proceed with your own learning.
4. *Fear of losing control.* If your boss asks for details, say, "I've delegated that to Patricia. I'll be happy to check with her and get you the answer this afternoon."
5. *Perfection complex.* "If it's worth doing, it's worth doing well." Loosen up. This idea, pursued blindly, leads to overcontrol and failure. Accept reasonable, adequate work in necessary routine areas. Recognize across-the-board perfection as a time waster.
6. *Lack of confidence in others.* Assume that, with your support, the project will be accomplished. Acknowledge the risks involved, and take steps to minimize them. Take the plunge.
7. *False efficiency.* "Takes me longer to show someone how to do this than to do it myself." So what if it takes Ignace two hours to do the job? Next time, he can do it faster. By assigning the job you bought yourself an extra half hour—time enough to do something far more valuable (that only you can do!).

When you get down to it, the "yes-buts" about delegating fall apart. Real managers know delegation is a time saver.

INVEST TIME, DON'T SPEND IT

Moses, having led his people out of Egypt, was so impressed with his own knowledge and authority that he insisted on ruling on every controversy personally. His father-in-law, a wise priest named Jethro, recognized this as poor use of a leader's time. Said Jethro: "Thou wilt surely wear away, both thou, and this people that is with thee: for this thing is too heavy for thee; thou art not able to perform it thyself alone." Jethro recommended that Moses select capable leaders and give them full authority over routine matters, thus freeing Moses to concentrate on major decisions and long-range plans.

The key to delegation is the word *entrust.* When you delegate, you entrust the entire matter to the other person, along with sufficient authority to make it work.

Bob Spinale, a modern prophet, leads his force of 13 in wholesaling chimney products for both fossil-fuel and gas applications. Spinale, general manager of Z-Flex, Inc., Manchester, New Hampshire, believes in investing time in delegation—with special attention to telephone training.

"Sure, we're based in New Hampshire but we talk by telephone with our sales reps, distributors, and large HVAC customers every day. We'll always do that. Our mission is to make time for the *important* calls—to get the routine calls handled effectively as they occur."

Communications technology is wonderful but perilous, says Spinale: "Fax and voice mail are fine in their place. But keep them in their place." Putting your best buyers through the taped third degree ("If you want service, press one *now*; if you want sales, press two *now*") is "demeaning and silly," he says. "That high-tech-takes-over sound will never happen here. I'm happy our competitors do it. Just one more way we're ahead."

Spinale *invests* time training office people to handle routine calls. He emphasizes each call's importance—in both sales and service areas. When the customer goes away aware of Class A treatment, Spinale knows that (1) time spent delegating the calls is paying off big, and (2) Spinale's own time has been preserved for calls only he can handle. "So the best way to *save* time is to *invest* time wisely in training employees in courteous, knowledgeable customer relations," he says.

PRIORITY-ACTIVATED DELEGATING

Does this mean delegate all things? Certainly not! Delegate to people who understand (naturally or through training) your philosophy, your objectives, and your strategies. If you delegate to those who do not share these qualities, you abdicate.

Evaluate delegating risk by asking yourself: "What's the *worst* that can go wrong?" If the worst is truly bad, monitor the project closely or don't delegate at all. When you do delegate, allow time cushions. If something unexpected goes haywire, you have time to correct it. Set up project checkpoints that allow subordinates to fail without losing the farm. Build in time to correct errors. Both you and employees learn from the experience.

Faced with an overly cautious subordinate ("too many questions, too often"), a manager told his assistant to "bring me three solutions to each question—rates 1–2–3 by preference." It worked. "She always came up with the right answers, instilling confidence in herself and trust in her abilities," he said.

Postdelegation, insist on being informed at each checkpoint. But do not interfere unless you feel very strongly. When you must reverse an employee's decision, come right out with it.

TIME NUGGETS: THE FOUR RULES OF DELEGATING

1. Be patient. People who take on jobs need time to learn.

2. Assign work gradually. Do not expect a subordinate to assume total responsibility overnight.

3. Try to delegate in advance. Avoid dropping a crash problem in a subordinate's lap.

4. Assign an entire job, not parts, whenever possible. It reduces confusion and errors.

Don't stand on ceremony. Pull rank. Sound brutal? Not so. It'll cause less rancor than prolonged discussion and argument.

On minor decisions, if a recommendation seems more or less in order, approve it. If it's marginal, give qualified approval, but ask that other alternatives be explored. If you totally disagree with the recommendation, throw it out. On important approvals, accept only excellence. The magic phrase, "Is this the best you can do?" usually works wonders.

AND HOW ABOUT YOUR BOSS?

Suppose you're gung ho on delegation, know and applaud its principles, but face one problem: Your boss doesn't. And you're the delegatee.

You may be partially at fault. Do you passively accept poor delegation, incomplete instructions, too many projects at a time, unclear deadlines? Make it easier on yourself via these eight steps:

1. On each assignment, find out how much authority you've got. Once you clarify authority, carry out the project without step-by-step approval.
2. Offer your boss solutions to other problems that arise while you're doing assigned work. It will strengthen your working relationship.
3. Repeat directions in your own words so you and your boss are certain you understand the assignment.
4. Ask for specific deadlines for each major segment.
5. If your boss procrastinates, write up your proposed action plan and say: "Dear Boss, unless I hear otherwise from you by such and such a date, I will go ahead and . . ."
6. If your boss dumps everything on you at the last minute, show him or her your To–Do List. Ask what the additional items will displace.
7. If your boss overwhelms you with work, ask him or her to prioritize tasks.
8. Ask how *well* the job needs to be done. A dollar's worth of effort on a penny project doesn't make sense.

CHAPTER 11

COMMUNICATIONS: TIME-SAVING PLUS OR BORING MINUS?

"Before you give someone a piece of your mind, make sure you can get by on what's left."

—Old New England Adage

Effective communication gets the job done with a *minimum* of repetition and misunderstanding. Poor communication often takes more time to get less done. Worse, the job may not get done at all. As business folklore tells it: "There may not always be time to do it. But there's *always* time to do it over."

HOW TO SPEAK RIGHT

When you're making a formal speech, your time management responsibilities increase greatly. As syndicated columnist Jenkin Lloyd Jones says: "A speech is a solemn responsibility. A bad 30-minute speech to 200 people wastes only a half hour of the speaker's time. But it wastes 100 hours of the audience's time—more than 4 days—which should be a hanging offense."

Get Into Your Audience's Shoes

Utilize time effectively. Think the way they think. It takes some doing. You've mastered your presentation; you deliver it impressively; but your prospect may be unable to assimilate the facts, especially in high-tech areas:

I know you believe you understand
what you think I said.
But I am not sure you realize that
what you heard is not what I meant.

That gives you reason to analyze receptivity of your audience, again and again.

Be Brief, Be Brief, Be Brief

As columnist Sidney Harris says: "Everyone is a bore on some subjects. The genuine bore is tedious on the subjects he knows best." That means you must use clear, simple words and statements that anyone can understand. Even the educated person appreciates simplicity of speech. Let terminology fit the slow thinker as well as the fast. A person who doesn't understand cannot be convinced.

Men and women who cultivate brevity are rare and refreshing. Brevity is a developed art. Can you summarize your product's or service's benefit in a dramatic, compelling sentence? No? Better start working on it. Sales manager Sonny Harris puts it bluntly:

> *Tell me quick and tell me true,*
> *Or else, my friend, the hell with you!*
> Less *of how your product came to be,*
> *And* more *of what it does for me!*

To Be Effective, Communication Must Be Believable

In business, as in life, presenter believability is critical. Unless you are believed, nothing makes a difference to the listener. Thus true interpersonal communication skills are the ability to build credibility and believability into what you *say* and *write*—and to do this within an effective time frame.

Communication that lacks credibility is a shameful waste of time. That's why Lee Stanley, president of Solar Additions, Inc., Greenwich, New York, considers command presence vital in "trying to accomplish objectives by using the English language."

"In the Army, I learned that if you talk, and some people listen, that's command presence. If you talk and nobody listens, you don't have it. The Army considers effective speech absolutely necessary for leadership. Orders must be executed accurately and *on time*."

Stanley's advice: "Learn to avoid *ums* and *ahs* in speech. At

Toastmasters chapter meetings they appoint an *ah* counter to note every time the speaker says *ah*. If you log 37 *ahs* in your address it gives you a clue: You're wasting time and boring your listeners."

Say It With Style

Quality speech and content are obligatory. But don't forget style. Be *interesting*. Here are ways:

- Speak journalistically to save time. Start with most important facts; work down to lesser facts and details. In presentation, tell what you're going to cover. Then live up to your promise. Then summarize.
- Work for distinctiveness. Develop a style that's pure *you*. Say it with *panache*. Often the way you say it makes it memorable—or appropriate. Or acceptable. Or believable.
- Speak with enthusiasm—that's knowledge on fire. At times, draw on *command presence,* and *eloquence*.
- Use the active voice. Don't waste words or time—both are in finite supply. Make each word pull its weight.
- Speak out with boldness and courage. Society is run by decision makers.
- Choose the familiar word rather than the technical, the concrete rather than the abstract, the direct rather than the circumlocution. Choose the vivid over the noncommittal, the specific over the general, the unusual over the trite.

Effective speech is a self-fulfilling prophecy. Word-wasting speakers do not sound authoritative and rarely achieve authority posts.

Wrapping It Up

Why priority-powered speech? The great entertainers have it. Top executives have it. Super salesfolk have it. Virtually every successful person utilizes effective speech. You can have it, too.

When you master effective speech you rivet and hold attention. You sell your opinions, ideas, products, yourself. As you acquire effective speech, barriers start to crumble. Goals you thought impossible become reachable. You feel positive, confident, secure—at social or business gatherings, large or small.

Conversation is more enjoyable. Others pay attention. Interruptions are reduced. People care about your opinions and views. Good speech tells your boss: "This person is born to command!"

You'll chair committees, lead groups, speak publicly. Your listeners, conditioned by screen, stage, and novels, judge your background and probable future by *what* you say and *how* you say it. Sterling speech moves you upward.

Importance of Two-Way Communications

After you issue verbal instructions, check to see if the transmission is clean and accurate. (The likelihood of accurate transmission is only fair.) Here's where careful checking is an effective time investment.

Ask for feedback. Don't assume anything. Take that extra minute to make sure communication is clear. It can save you hours of misunderstandings later. Feedback strengthens communications. You'll be surprised at the discrepancies between what you *think* you said and what others *think* they heard.

After you issue instructions, ask the listener to repeat "just to be sure I've explained it clearly!" Conversely, when you're a victim of poor communication, say: "I want to be sure I understand you clearly; what you want is . . ."

Don't Forget to Listen!

Since communication is by definition two-way, you must listen or scuttle its value. (The ratio of *one* mouth to *two* ears is often cited as memory aid.) Remember, people—including you—often listen with psychological filters, hearing what they want to.

To spruce up the listening end of two-way transmission:

- Give your full attention to what's being said. Stop everything else you're doing. Maintain eye contact.

- Don't let tone of voice, nervousness, or misplaced emotions cloud the message. Distill out the content.
- Prepare beforehand by reading information pertinent to the discussion. This helps you evaluate both speaker and subject.
- Place disturbing interruptions in context. Judge what the speaker says given the conditions.
- Avoid getting sidetracked. Listen particularly closely to points you *disagree* with. (Poor listeners shut out or distort them.)
- Mentally collect the main points of the conversation. Occasionally, for clarification, repeat one of the speaker's statements. It shows interest and helps the speaker better organize thoughts.
- At the end of the talk, restate what you've heard.

WHEN TO WRITE RIGHT

With many communications opportunities, your best bet is to not say anything. Write instead.

The Memo

Use the powerful hand-written memo. Keep your notepaper small so you can't write too much! *"But you were just great—I am forever in your debt"* is worth at least six paragraphs of typed sweet nothings.

- Make notes brief, almost telegraphic, when asking for or giving instructions.
- Write your message by hand. Edit the draft. Make it short, clear, and reflective of your personality (not the language of the bureaucrat or junior clerk).
- Come to the point, instantly. Cut all waffle. Put everything in the briefest possible way. Use colorful words (they often take the place of whole paragraphs and make your copy memorable).

The hand-written memo is far and away the most effective method of communication (quicker and more decisive than a meeting—even a one-on-one meeting). It beats the telephone most of the time. You call *A,* who's in a meeting. You leave your number. She calls back—you're in a meeting. You call again—she's out of town. She returns your call—you're holding an important interview. You talk inconclusively and promise to send a note. Why not *start* that way?

Faxed memos are more efficient than telephone calls and command more immediate attention.

When you send out a memo, address it only to the person who must act upon it. Others concerned get FYI (for your information) copies. Address a round-robin request to several people and you get time-wasting confusion. Either nobody will respond or you'll get as many conflicting responses as you have names.

Taping for Transcription

If you read time management advice (and obviously you do), you know the experts recommend dictating as a way of getting your work done without going crazy.

Don't get us wrong. We advocate generating as little paperwork as possible. When you *can* speak directly, do. Oral

TIME NUGGETS: TIME-SAVING WRITING TIPS

- **Write responses in the margin of the letter you receive and mail it back to the sender. Saves filing a copy, too.**
- **Eliminate unnecessary words, sentences, paragraphs—there's nothing wrong with one-paragraph letters.**
- **Think before you write. Then use short and simple words.**
- **Don't overrevise in the name of perfection. Added benefits may be small or nonexistent.**

communication is fast, efficient, useful. In many cases, though, you need writing—for accuracy, a permanent record, chapter-and-verse details.

So when you do need to tape for transcription, here's how. Some normally articulate people are at a total loss verbalizing their thoughts. True, enormous amounts of time and money are wasted by putting words you *don't need* on tape—dross that must later be expunged and then processed at more cost.

The solution: Start with only the words you need on tape. Easier said than done? Perhaps. But these principles will help.

If you have a hard time getting started, begin by reading aloud into the microphone. Gradually, you'll begin to feel more comfortable. Soon you'll be able to make the transition reading-to-recording. Set a time each day and practice dictating at least 15 minutes. For most, morning hours are best. Let nothing interfere. You're forming a habit. Make sure you sound like a human being, not a machine. Use everyday language, not gobbledygook.

Picture the person you're writing. See that person sitting across from you. It'll show up in the copy. Once your words are flowing, keep going. Pause and collect your thoughts, but don't let your mind go fishing.

Before you start, jot (on incoming correspondence) a skeleton outline of your intended response—a few words or phrases. Then, on mike, use these notes as a springboard. Tape answers immediately. Beware of waiting for a "more convenient" time.

Organize before you start. Stack number one requires a quick response. Start taping answers as soon as you're able. Stack number two requires an answer, but no urgency. Stack number three requires research. Hold response until you gather facts. Letters that require no answer don't get in the stack. The more you toss the better. With data in hand, you'll soon tape smooth, conversational sentences. Your words will show your mastery.

Alas: Hand-written won't always do. In some cases a memo or letter must be written. Thus the composition.

The Composition

Don't sit down to write that important letter or report until you know exactly what you want to say. To stare at blank paper is a terrible waste of time. Make an outline first. Write yourself a telegram. Put down, in not more than 20 words, a crisp statement of what the writing will cover. List the main points: one item per line. Number the items by importance (most important is number one, etc.).

Once you're satisfied the outline is up to scratch, hang meat on the bones. Remember, you are not writing a detective story; don't keep your reader in suspense. And don't struggle with exact wording. Polish during the editing phase, after you give it a chance to cool for a while.

If the reader is unknown, establish your credentials as early as possible. Prove your opinions are worth reading and heeding. What does your reader want or need from you? What desires can you help fulfill? Try to determine the reader's occupation, educational background, level of interest, age, and sex. All these items help establish that you put yourself in the reader's shoes.

When you get to the purpose or main text, here are two ways to advance your argument:

1. Lead off with your strongest point, followed by your weakest argument, and close with the next-to-strongest argument.
2. Begin with a strong argument, but not the best one. Follow with a weaker argument. Close out with the strongest argument of all. Be brief, be forceful, do not drag in extraneous ideas. Don't let the reader's attention lag.

After the final point, ask the reader for action.

PART

CONTROLLING YOUR TOOLS

CHAPTER 12

THE TELEPHONE: TOOL OR TIME THIEF?

"You delay but time does not."

—Ben Franklin

One discovery shocking to the new time logger: the high percentage of each day spent on the telephone! Two to four hours of a normal workday is typical on accurate time logs (and only *accurate* sheets propel you into priority-activated time management).

Yet the telephone, viewed in a vacuum, is a marvel. In the acclaimed television series *The Ascent of Man*, Jacob Bronowski called the telephone "one of mankind's superb inventions." Indeed, our global society depends utterly upon the telephone. In the 1991 crisis in the Soviet Union, President Bush picked up the telephone many times each day to talk personally to world leaders. (Contrast this with the transatlantic ship that carried news of the War of 1812 peace treaty. It arrived in North America many months after the fact—nowhere near in time to preclude the Battle of New Orleans.)

"Sure we can't live *without* the telephone," one textile manager said. "But we can't live *with* it either. It's a monster."

The non–time manager may well conclude that. But priority-activated managers can become the telephone's master. For starters, view this "superb instrument" as fraternal twins: *incoming* and *outgoing*.

CONTROLLING THE INCOMING MONSTER

To understand why the incoming telephone gets such a grip on you, review the power of human nature. Recognize this power, but don't let it cripple you. The telephone is not a humanoid with a life of its own. It is a valuable tool for communication—no less, but definitely no more.

Sure, there's something irresistible about the imperious tone of the ring: "Pick me up. I may have important news for you." In a work setting, probably not one person in a thousand can ignore it. Yet tame it you must, for telephone interruptions can fracture your productivity like nothing else.

You say: "But I *must* take these calls. It might be my boss or our big client, someone who *needs* me." Remember, the problem is not just the amount of time the interruption uses up, but the amount of time you need to catch up mentally to where you were before.

What do you do when you're out of the office? Don't you make arrangements for your calls to be taken—and your callers served? Well, why can't you do the same when you're *in* the office? (I can hear you saying, "Yes, but . . .") Agreeing intellectually is easier than agreeing viscerally. Be honest and check off visceral objections that apply to you:

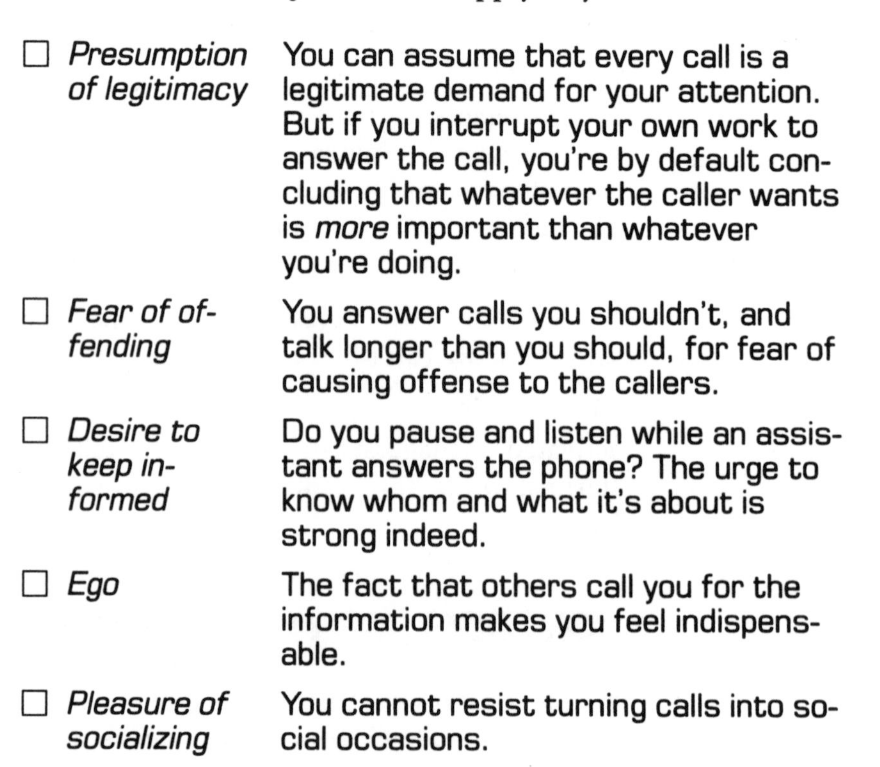

☐ *Presumption of legitimacy*	You can assume that every call is a legitimate demand for your attention. But if you interrupt your own work to answer the call, you're by default concluding that whatever the caller wants is *more* important than whatever you're doing.
☐ *Fear of offending*	You answer calls you shouldn't, and talk longer than you should, for fear of causing offense to the callers.
☐ *Desire to keep informed*	Do you pause and listen while an assistant answers the phone? The urge to know whom and what it's about is strong indeed.
☐ *Ego*	The fact that others call you for the information makes you feel indispensable.
☐ *Pleasure of socializing*	You cannot resist turning calls into social occasions.

☐ *A handy excuse* — Reluctant to take up a difficult (or boring) task, answering "important" phone calls provides you with a wonderful rationale for procrastinating.

Surprised at how many apply to you? Now attack the problem. The first defense: Not always being there—it's called *screening*.

HOW TO MANAGE SCREENING

Screening involves setting aside two time blocks a day to return calls—say, 11:00 to noon and 4:00 to 4:45 P.M. Few calls suffer from a callback the next day. (The 1 percent that require instant action? Call back in ten minutes. With proper prioritizing, there won't be many.) With your screener, decide which categories of calls you want to accept right away: family, the boss, company VIPs, major clients. Define "emergency." For all others, your screener will take callback messages. Then honor your regular time blocks for returning calls.

Caution: Screening doesn't mean insulting the caller. Your own unfortunate calling experiences may have turned you off of

TIME NUGGETS: FOUR TIPS ON SCREENING

1. **Whenever possible, screener answers the caller's question, arranges for the material, takes down the information, and handles the request if feasible.**
2. **Unable to handle the call, screener tries to refer the caller to someone else in the organization who can help.**
3. **If only you can handle the call, screener takes a message so you can return call.**
4. **If call meets your preset emergency or VIP guidelines, the screener puts the call through.**

screening. But a skilled, properly trained assistant can deflect interruptions without offending callers.

Often a polite, businesslike approach is sufficient: "I'm sorry, she's not available at this moment. May she call you back? May I add a brief note telling her what this is about?"

I can see the gleam in your eye. "I don't have an assistant. Ha! Won't work for me." Sure it will. Here are some ways:

- Work out a deal with your colleagues. You cover their telephones for a while; they cover yours.
- Simply unplug the phone during critical work periods. The caller, hearing unanswered rings, assumes you're away from your desk.
- Take your work and go somewhere in the building where there are no phones.

Suppose you're in your boss's office or a colleague's, and you're interrupted by an incoming call for him or her. Of course, you do *not* control the screening. Two solutions:

1. Write on a piece of paper: "I see you're busy. I'll go back to my desk and continue on the XYZ project I'm working on for you. Give me a buzz when you're free." Place it on his or her desk, and leave.
2. After the call is over, say: "Do you think Ellen could hold your calls for a bit? I think we can finish this in five minutes."

TAMING THE OUTGOING MONSTER

You're doing incoming right. Your assistant screens your calls, and it's time for callbacks. First, collect the files and backup information you need, then check your notes from your last conversation with each caller. Make sure you have some routine work handy—signing mail, for instance—in case you are put on hold. But don't allow yourself to be put on hold—*unless* you're calling an extraordinarily difficult-to-reach person (whereupon staying on the line will be a time saver in the long run).

If the person you're calling is not in, find out when he or she will be available, and don't call at any other time. Make an appointment to call at that specific time and leave word concerning what you're calling about so that the call can proceed smoothly.

When your call goes through, try to complete it within six minutes. Most calls shouldn't last more than two minutes. Your first sentence will set the tone: businesslike, or social chit-chat:

No: "Hello, Eileen. How's the weather in Augusta?"
Yes: "Hello, Eileen, this is Jeff. I know you're busy this morning. I just have one quick question about the Santa Fe contract."

If you ask about her family, she'll feel obliged to ask about *your* family, and both will have wasted time.

Randy Giles, CEO of Hearthstone Homes, in Dandridge, Tennessee, uses a pleasant, businesslike opening when he returns a call: "Hello, George! What's up?" This tone indicates genuine interest coupled with a need to get on with it. As a result, he accomplishes much each day.

TIME NUGGETS: TIPS ON CALLING

- **Inform everyone who calls you from now on the best time to reach you.**
- **Set aside the same time segment each day for callbacks.**
- **Place an egg timer by your telephone. Limit your calls to three minutes. You won't think this is silly when you see how well it works.**
- **Prepare a put-through/take-message list for your screener. Put it in code, just in case . . .**

After you've completed the call's mission, particularly if the person you're speaking with shows no signs of lagging, say:

- "Wait, before we hang up, I want to be sure we're clear about this one point."
- "I just have a minute before I have to leave for a meeting, Bob. Was there anything else you need?"

HIGH-TECH, LOW-TECH, NO-TECH

If you want to utilize your assistant for nonscreening functions—or if you don't have an assistant—the age of technology beckons:

- *Telephone answering machines* take your calls while you're out, or enable you to listen to incoming calls and decide whether or not to answer.
- *Cordless phones* allow you to carry on a conversation while walking about the office or building.
- *Automatic dialing* stores frequently called numbers. To dial, push one or two code numbers. Automatic redial allows you to redial the last number you called by hitting the redial button. If the number is busy, the unit redials at programmed intervals.
- *Speakerphones* enable you to talk to the other party without holding the phone to your ear—freeing you to do other things.
- *Call forwarding* automatically forwards your incoming calls to a new number you've designated. You never miss a call this way.
- *Call waiting* signals someone else is trying to reach you when you're on the phone.
- *Conference calls* allow you to talk long distance with several parties, thus eliminating time-consuming travel. Check with the conference call operator for details.

Be it by better methods, trained assistance, new technology—or all three—you can get closer to Somerset Maugham's idea of heaven: "Where the blessed use the telephone for what they have to say and not a word besides."

CHAPTER 13

OPERATE YOUR WORK STATION OR IT'LL OPERATE YOU

"Next to the dog, the wastebasket is your best friend."

—B. C. Forbes

James A. Grinder, New York public relations character, once announced—in all seriousness—he'd discovered the perfect way to solve the burgeoning paper problem.

"Take everything in your In-Box and put it in your Out-Box," Grinder said. "It goes away and takes three days to get back!"

We thought he was kidding—until we caught him actually doing it!

All too many antipaper plans are either like Grinder's (delaying the inevitable while holding up work) or overagonizing (solving problem A but sticking you with problem B in the process). There are, however, techniques to guide you between *The Rock and the Hard Place*. Listen up:

View Paper as Fluid

When you start thinking of paper as fluid—some see it as a sewer analogy—you're on the right track. Water that sits becomes stagnant and murky, takes on green film, attracts bugs. So does paper. Not only do *you* have to "go with the flow," so does the paper.

Handle the flow quickly—more often, straight into the trash. Never send someone paper just to get it off your desk. Have the courage to deep-six it.

To encourage the flow, read everything as it falls into your hands. Act on issues that can be dealt with—immediately. Don't shuffle papers. Don't put them in piles. When you get a memo, a letter, or a document, your first instinct should be to throw it away. Most people keep ten times more than they need.

If you can't throw it away, skim it and decide on action. Make informative marginal comments. *Yes. No. Agree. Good. See me. Let's discuss. You decide. What do you think?* The good manager can get a great deal of feeling into: *Well done. Over my dead body. Sensational. Stupid. Bravo! Come off it!* If a document requires no comment, throw it away. Most paper marked *file* should get the deep six instead.

All bills for approval go forward for payment or back to the supplier for adjustment. Don't hold bills, *ever.* Don't file bills before they're paid!

Make sure you have an empty In-Box three or four times a day—and *always* at night. You're permitted a full Hold-Box containing problems too difficult to solve immediately. Go through it once a day. You'll find many previously intractable problems have solved themselves.

Give priority classifications to your memos or letters. If you require immediate action, label it *immediate.* If secret, call it *secret. Private* and *personal* work only if staff has been instructed not to open mail so marked. Don't bother with *confidential*—it's lost all meaning.

Contrary to what many said in the early high-tech days, computers don't create *less* paperwork—they create *more and more* faddish paper, reams of useless reports, uncounted pieces of junk mail, and meaningless documents.

Now that practically every office has a fax machine, the mountain of paperwork is getting taller at a much faster rate. Copies of reports and memoranda circulate widely; few question the need. Top management is bombarded with documents from several levels down, and lower levels find themselves submerged with route-downs from topside.

View Paper as Expense

Each extra sheet costs money: the handling, reading, reporting, and (God save the mark!) filing. Every sheet you eliminate *saves* money.

Worse than monetary costs: the needless waste of time/energy created by this plethora of paper. It costs time to fill out forms, write memos, read computer printouts, prepare budgets, write orders, make 14 copies, and read junk mail.

"Skim and dispose" is one manager's solution to executive reading. He's aware that one popular way to squander time is called "acquiring information." Sure, there's an ocean of material you must go through. You just can't read it all. Time experts have no patience with the manager who reads *Business Week* or *Fortune* or *The Wall Street Journal* page by page. Scan. Suck all the nourishment out. Then throw the rest away.

In a magazine, go to the table of contents first and pick out the things important to you—and read those. In a newspaper, scan the headlines. Extract the essence and let the rest go.

Business is a world of changing priorities. The successful climber adjusts those priorities every day, every month, every minute. As you get higher, you must know more and more about what's going on. At each step up you've got to be better informed. Figure out a way to get this information and not go crazy in the process. (If that sounds like a tall order, it helps explain why the apex is so narrow at the top.)

Sure, there are speed-reading courses. Probably speed-*skimming* would be more useful. Not long ago, a well-organized manager ran through a copy of *Nation's Business*. He tore out two articles to read. He routed one to somebody else. He ignored a topic he was interested in last week but not interested in today. He resisted the temptation to read an amusing article (he didn't need entertainment at that point). Then he threw the magazine in the wastebasket—not to be bothered with wastepaper.

Said consultant James A. Newman: "I do that with *The New York Times* and *The Wall Street Journal* every day. Every three days on the average, I'll pull something out and direct it to somebody else."

Read and clip and *get rid of paper*. The advertising manager for a large business machines division felt he should read *The Wall Street Journal*—every word. But he never did. So his office suffered from three months of stacked-up journals. He said: "I'm going to read them." Of course he never did.

Clear the decks every day. At day's end on a daily newspaper, the editors throw everything away. They know they're going to get a lot more the next morning. They just can't cope with residue. Everything unused goes in the wastebasket. This causes some problems. But it also sustains life.

Keep your paper under control. The wastebasket is your best friend. Even your pet cocker spaniel can't help with paper.

VALUES OF SELECTIVE READING

Do you feel swamped by the amount of material you must read? Many do. Is there a way out of the jungle of letters, reports, periodicals, and books that absolutely must be read? Yes:

- *Establish reading goals.* They can be personal or professional, long or short term, but it's important that you know exactly what they are. Whether you're contemplating a trip to a trade show or convention, or trying to keep up-to-date with the latest industry breakthroughs, your reading should reflect these goals.
- *Be selective.* Would you eat everything in sight just to be well nourished? Of course not. Apply the same principle to reading. Be selective about what portions of books, magazines, and other materials you read. Choose those related to your goals. If you find the piece isn't pertinent or isn't telling you anything new, stop. In fact, you can eliminate a lot of reading material. Newspaper articles are written in inverted pyramid style. The first paragraph summarizes the story. Each succeeding paragraph provides more detail. Often the headlines and the first few paragraphs keep you well informed. In books and reports, skim the table of contents and index for nuggets that contribute to your goals. Whether you read the complete book or report depends entirely on how closely it's linked to your goals.
- *Set deadlines.* If you don't read the daily newspaper the day it's published, throw it out. The same applies to May's newsletter on June 1. Important topics are sure to be discussed again. As you read, underline, make margin notes, put ques-

tion marks by confusing statements. By marking you are outlining its main points. When you refer again, you won't need to reread the entire article. Still swamped? Try delegation. Enlist the help of a co-worker, spouse, friend, or relative. Ask them to read and summarize.

Beware the Friendly Copier

What a wonderful machine is the office copier! Booz Allen Hamilton, in helping a major TV network cut overhead, reduced 37 copying machines down to 13. The most important benefit—much more than the savings on machines and paper—was the executive time saved in not reading all that paper (most of it unnecessary).

Some people are copy fanatics. They make copies and send them all over the place—clogging up the flow. If you're going to run five copies, you think, "Why not run seven or eight?" Pretty soon you're drowning in your own clutter. The copying machine is a mixed blessing. When you need copies, it's good. Excess copying is a bitter enemy of priority-driven time management.

WHAT YOU *CAN* DO ABOUT PAPER

Tom Morrissey, a consultant on throwing away unneeded corporate papers, estimates that 95 percent of what "must be kept" should never have been filed in the first place. This means:

- Whenever you're tempted to document something, ask yourself: "What's the worst that can happen by not recording this?" If the answer isn't too bad, don't.
- If someone writes you requesting information, answer on the incoming letter.
- Prepare a short priority list of papers you need. Let your assistant screen out and handle the rest.
- Request your name off mailing and subscription lists.
- Think twice every time you consider keeping an extra copy. When in doubt, throw it out.

- Handle each paper once. Otherwise you'll expend double time and energy picking it up again.
- Remember that a long distance call often eliminates paper and saves time.
- Reward employees who suggest significant ways to reduce paper.
- Before reading something, ask: "Is this likely to move me toward my priority goals?" If not, throw it out.
- Never answer a letter that someone else can answer.
- Substitute oral for written reports.
- Ask for summaries instead of lengthy reports and get your assistant to mark key passages in reports.
- Take a speed-scanning course.

Commonsense Paper Management

People still make notes about memoing when writing the memo would've taken the same time. Remember the advice of Admiral Horatio Nelson: "Do it now. Do it *right* now."

Take a leaf from the notebook of Jack Chase, genial Hampton, Virginia, sales manager. Chase collects prospect cards at trade shows. At noon and each night he pastes each card on a single page of a school composition book. Clearly labeled on the book cover: name/date/location of trade show. On each page he uses the ample sheet to add notes about name/company/product. "This simple plan has saved me at least 50 hours of time at each trade show," Chase says. "And think of the time it saves in follow-up!" No wonder Jack Chase always appears to be on top of his customers and prospects. He is!

The Dump Drawer

One chief executive uses a 90-day drawer. All his mail goes into that drawer "to ripen." It's surprising how little has importance after 90 days, he says.

Designate one of your lower drawers as a dump drawer. Into this drawer put low-payoff, low-priority items—flyers, brochures, newspapers, other mail that isn't time-critical. Let them ripen for a month or so.

During the last hour on Fridays when it's not practical to begin major projects, hold a *trivia session.* Go through your dump drawer. Scan the items to decide: Toss, let ripen further, delegate, or do. Fully 90 percent of your dump drawer can be thrown out.

TAILOR SYSTEM TO SELF

In the final analysis, you must tailor your office system to your personality and temperament. Heed the words of William S. Gilbert:

> *What will satisfy B*
> *will quite scandalize C*
> *for C is so very particular!*

Ann McGee-Cooper, a Dallas consultant, marches to a different drummer. She keeps in step just fine, thank you. She says, don't turn *organization* into *obsession.*

"Those of us who are right-brain dominant, and thus visually motivated, function best with clutter," maintains McGee-Cooper. "We know where things are in those piles, and because we see them, we remember to take care of them. So for us, it's important to realize that too much organizing and too much filing can be a time waster."

Bill Persons, a North Carolina housing manufacturer, rebelled against keeping telephone numbers on computer. He explains: "My assistant can put a telephone number on screen in 3 minutes. I can find it in 30 seconds in my index card file. Who's ahead?"

Persons also says alphabetical order with simple telephone card files is "arrant nonsense." He uses his own "gravity-fed system." "After you take Sandy Smith's card out of the *S* section, put it away in *front* of the *S* group. Next time you go into the *S* system, you take out Jane Sort. Put her at the front. By their own gravity, frequently used cards gravitate to the front. Cards

TIME LAB PAPERWORK

	Roadblock	Rerouting
1.	Reading essentials	Scan for essentials. Take a speed-reading course to learn scanning. Assign assistant to summarize content.
2.	Leaving tasks unfinished	Complete tasks before putting them down.
3.	Perfectionism	"Is it adequate?" (not perfect) is your question on 80 percent of work.
4.	Not delegating	Paper follows responsibility that has been delegated. So delegate job *and* paper.
5.	Attempting too much at once	Be realistic. Others will be about you.
6.	Lack of system	Standardize forms; reduce report length and number where possible; screen selectively; delegate; control record retention.
7.	Overfiling	Answer on original. If filing is necessary 5 percent of the time, use back of original for copy of your response.
8.	Hoarding	Get rid of it; keep it moving. Learn to view hoarding as silly.
9.	Indecision	Scan it once, and handle it. Think of flow in a pipeline.

10. Procrastination	Do it now. Eighty percent of daily intake can be disposed of on first handling. The average manager disposes of only 20 percent.

you use once a year are further back. The more you use a card, the easier your access."

What about numbers called daily? "Well, I'm not against all automation," Persons says. "We have direct dialing, where codes are programmed into our phone system to allow us to reach frequently called numbers using only two digits. We keep that up to date. I'm just against high-tech when we're swatting a gnat with a two-by-four plank." The proper meld of high-tech and low-tech—leavened with common sense—saves office time for Bill Persons.

Follow-up files remind you of upcoming deadlines, things to do, and projects to follow up on. This special file, also called a tickler, has a set of 12 folders (one for each month of the year) and another set of 31 folders (for each day of the month). Place the current month first in the drawer with the days behind it.

At the beginning of each month, transfer items for that month into appropriate daily slots. File work in the tickler file according to when you want to begin it. For example, if you have a report due January 15, file the material under the date you wish to begin. If you have a bill due January 10, file it in the January 7 folder. If the materials are too bulky, slip a note into the slot. Follow-up files can also be useful for payment dates, birthdays, and anniversaries.

Rolltop Desk or Work Station: Mission's the Same

In an earlier era, the rolltop desk served as combined writing space and filing cabinet (leaving as legacy the expression *pigeonholed*—bills held up in Congress). Then came the file cabinet beside the smooth-top desk, followed by the steel or plastic slab and central files somewhere else.

Today we have the high-tech work station with seemingly enough hardware and software to launch the next Mars probe. But throughout this 100-year span one mission has remained constant: keeping an orderly work environment to serve its occupants. Not *frustrate, delay,* or *aggravate*—but *serve.*

Why is order so important? Since you spend many hours of your career in your work environment, it pays to keep it clear of clutter. In a clean and organized work area, you concentrate better, produce more, remember longer. When your work station works with you, you're more creative and your problem-solving abilities soar.

How do desks get so disorganized? Could be you have so many important things to do you're afraid to put them out of sight (you might forget them). Meanwhile, more important items get piled on top. Pieces of paper cry out, "Do me first!" "No, no, do me first! I'm an emergency, too." Working under these conditions is exhausting. You're spending valuable energy trying to ignore all that paper while attempting to solve the tasks at hand.

Now let's conduct an experiment. Take everything off your desk and put it out of sight in another room. Just look at it, devoid of clutter. Is it refreshing? If it makes you nervous, you may equate messiness with productivity. (The two are not the same. A cluttered desk tends to go with a cluttered mind.)

Now return your most recent project to the desktop—several file folders, a book or two, and forms; use whatever's related. The point: Working on one task at a time helps you to concentrate and think clearly.

Think of the joy of working on just one project on that clear, smooth surface! It can be that way each day. Physician, heal thyself! Converts to clean-deskism report savings of an hour a day and more.

PART

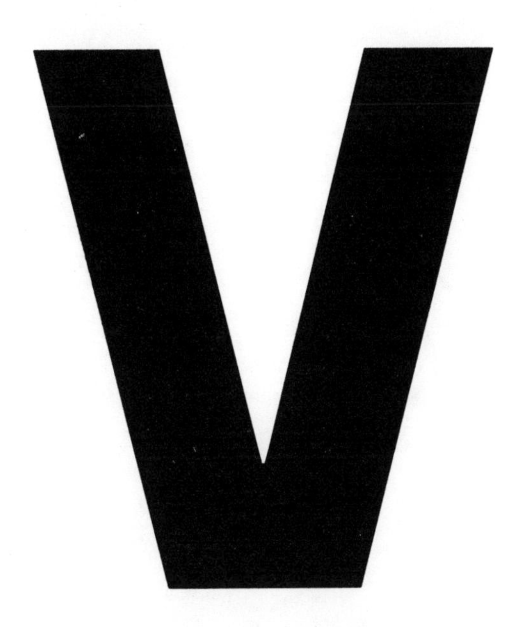

TAMING TRAVEL TIME

CHAPTER 14

THE ON-THE-GO MANAGER PRIORITIZES TRAVEL TIME

"But at my back I always hear Time's wingèd chariot hurrying near . . ."

—Andrew Marvell

Right after the 1991 Gulf War, a U.S. construction company hired a Middle East consultant—a Saudi native—to provide on-the-ground counsel. The mission: getting contracts to help rebuild Kuwait. The executive vice-president, just returned from Kuwait, told his CEO: "The only trouble is, now I need to sit down with Abdul for four days. Even though I've just come back, looks like I have to go again!"

The CEO held up his hand. "Maybe you don't. Invite *him* to come *here*. Cost is the same. Gives you time to catch your breath. And he'd probably like to visit America for the first time."

It worked. The construction people got to meet their new teammate. Abdul enjoyed the trip. The harried American saved two days of travel—wise deployment of time. You don't *always* need to go. Sometimes it works better if *they* come to *you*.

Consider asking your client to come to your offices, where detailed information is available plus facilities to make a full presentation. Insurance agents and securities account executives who practice this save one or two hours a day. Further, when appointments get cancelled, they are in their own offices, where time otherwise lost can be plowed back into productive use immediately.

Other solutions to the "must" trip are:

- *Send someone else.* A junior associate, attending as your representative, can often do well and get an invaluable learning experience. If the subject involves someone else's specialty, why not send the specialist?

- *Use other communications.* Can you accomplish your purpose with a letter or a call? A videoconference can avoid several people traveling all day for a one-hour discussion.
- *Postpone.* Don't overreact and go rushing off. Wait till you have all the facts. Don't schedule the meeting if a key decision maker isn't available. If it isn't urgent, wait till a more convenient time. Suggest: "I'll be in your area in ten days. Can it wait till then?"

If You Do Go, Go Right

Once you determine the trip is necessary now, look for ways to mine the most from your time. Plan the start–to–return itinerary for time management. Where possible, try to group appointments together. Who else can you visit on the same trip? Can other subjects be discussed? On layovers, schedule appointments at airports, make phone calls, or read valuable (but not pressing) materials. Take a portable office (writing materials, calculator, tape recorder, laptop computer) along.

Make sure your appointment schedule includes home numbers, in case plans change. Leave standing instructions with your travel agent; avoid arriving or departing during local rush hours. Naturally, insist on flight numbers, meal service, departure and arrival times, ground transportation details, and hotel reservations (addresses, phone numbers, reservation numbers). Get advance weather data so you can dress for cold/hot weather destinations. Hold luggage to carry-on, to save much time and stress on arrival.

Don't automatically get a plane. Often driving 150 miles or less is a better choice (avoid ticket lines, waiting rooms, flight delays, airline food, lost baggage).

Don't drive to the airport: Cab or limo avoids the parking hassle. Use highway time for reading or catching your breath. When you make a mad dash to the plane, you'll be tempted to sink back and relax once you sit down, instead of working. Use preboarding minutes to make phone calls or mentally rehearse your presentation. Don't overlook the tidbits of time. Ten minutes may not sound significant, but six ten-minute segments add up to an hour.

On economy flights, ask for an aisle seat. Get a left-side aisle seat so your writing arm is on the outside (left-handers should sit on the right-side aisle). Then watch for a change spot next to an empty seat (better for work). If you're traveling with an associate you need to confer with, do. Otherwise explain you need quiet time in a separate seat in order to work.

Prearrange your in-flight folders by color code—the number one priority on top. Once you arrive, ship completed work back to your assistant (using prestamped envelopes). Or if you're using a laptop or portable computer, plug into a hotel telephone and unload your machine into your assistant's computer. If you arrange it so, travel time is uninterrupted work time. No phone, no casual visitors, no meetings, and if there is a crisis, someone else takes care of it!

"Cars, trains, and airplanes are ideal for writing and reading," one ad manager says. "When I arrive back from a trip, I have office papers delivered to the airport. By the time I get to the office, I've looked at most of them, and dealt with the most urgent. Airplanes are sensational for report writing—safe from interruptions. Try to travel alone. Don't watch the movie."

Traveling legislators agree. "I doubt there was ever a time a congressman could feel well informed on every issue before him," says Congressman John Rhodes of Arizona. "We're at a point where we're less informed about more and more that comes before us." There's no easy answer, he says, so he makes do. "I'm blessed because I'm from Arizona, and it takes six or seven hours to get there from D.C.," he says. "I never get on an airplane without a briefcase full of papers."

When you get to the hotel, resist pressures to go out on the town if you really aren't interested. Work or rest instead. Don't feel obligated. Carefully consider the purpose of evening activity and act accordingly.

Don't eat excessively. Abundant food makes you sluggish. On a trip an amazing amount of alcohol can go down the hatch: at the airport, on the plane (before and after dinner), following your arrival, a few more in the evening, a nightcap. Most people can't take it. If you don't wind up drunk, you'll at least be seriously debilitated—when you need to perform at peak.

TIME LAB
MAKE EFFECTIVE USE OF COMMUTING TIME

- How much daily time do you spend commuting? Get a weekly figure. Multiply by 50 weeks and you get a large chunk of time! Use this time wisely. With proper planning, you can accomplish a lot.
- Plan commuting activities in advance on your daily To–Do List. Choose a long-term need (new subject, a foreign language, educational tape). Listen to tapes every day as you travel.
- Rehearse speeches and presentations.
- Write business letters, friendly notes, memos.
- Consider flextime at work. Come in earlier and leave earlier, or come in later and leave later. You thus avoid rush hour.
- If driving, don't weave in and out of traffic to get to work ten minutes earlier. The time you save isn't worth the stress and pressure. Get to work (or home) with energy and sanity intact.
- A phone in your car may be a reasonable investment. Carry a small portable tape recorder and make notes while traffic is stalled.

Before You Go and After You Return

Before you depart, ask your team members this question: "What will you have accomplished when I return?" Responses are both a goal and a commitment. Announce a set time you'll call the office each day. When you return, deal immediately with notes from the trip (expense reports, ideas collected). If necessary, spend the first day in a hideaway. If you procrastinate ("I'll just do that tomorrow"), by the time you get to it, you'll forget details and lose value.

CHAPTER 15

MARCH OF TIME IN THE GLOBAL VILLAGE

"Even if you're on the right track, you'll get run over if you just sit there."

—American Railroad Saying

A few short years back, Marshall McLuhan predicted the global village. Most managers then thought: "He means a century down the road."

He *didn't.* It's here today. Ask Arthur M. Pappas.

Pappas, head man for Asia and Latin America at Glaxo PLC, a British pharmaceutical company, this past year spent 43 days in London, 63 in Singapore, 47 in Raleigh, North Carolina, 22 in other U.S. states, and 123 in other countries. Pappas figures the 20 round-the-globe managers who report to him are "on a more intimate discussion basis" with him because of his extensive travel. That calls for global time management techniques unheard of even in the 1980s.

But, you say, the interlink world computer system and the wonderful fax make it easier. Not so, says Leonard Liu. "You cannot use a computer to do critical decision making in a group," says Liu, president of Taiwanese computer maker Acer Group and CEO of its U.S. unit in San Jose, California.

Liu says he often talks to managers in Europe at 6:30 A.M. from his San Francisco home. Evenings, he may confer with Taipei well into the night, again from home. His travel schedule leaves him only ten days a month in the city, where his wife and eight-year-old son live. "We are trying to globalize the company and get the people in local areas to work closely with each other," he says. "I make myself the bridge."

But Liu does draw the line. No telephone in his car. His 40-minute home-to-office drive is a "decompression period." A spouse who keeps a semblance of regularity at home helps.

"My wife is the boss," he says. "When I'm not around, things don't wait to be taken care of."

If you're the buyer, a seller will often call you during *your* office hours. But when you're the seller, guess who finds herself making midnight calls? Example: Joanne de Asis—who juggles time zones.

At least two nights a week, she talks with CS First Boston clients in Asia. If she's trying to close a deal, she may not get to sleep until 3:00 A.M. In the afternoon, when Asia is still asleep, she takes care of personal business. "Because of my odd hours," she says, "I skip out at 3:00 in the afternoon for a parent-teacher meeting or whatever." But, de Asis says, it's hard to plan dinner with friends or visit her large family. Recently, she had to close a deal from the ladies' room of the Met, where she was watching the Bolshoi.

As more companies go global, executives—if they aren't traveling abroad—are working late or getting interrupted at home by calls and faxes from other time zones. Most managers accept midnight phone calls and computer messages as part of being global. "It's second nature for me," says John E. Davies, who heads Ecogen, Inc., a biological pesticide start-up based in Langhorne, Pennsylvania. "I'm as used to it as I would be if I took the bus every morning."

When Baldwin Technology, a parts maker for the printing industry, sharply increased its overseas business, the travel schedule of its chairman/CEO jumped, too. Wendell Smith now spends only a fifth of his time at the headquarters in Rowayton, Connecticut, compared with 50 percent five years ago. "When you're growing at the rate we are, you cannot integrate acquisitions or make changes" sitting at the home office, Smith says.

What new time-taming techniques are arising to meet global needs? Charles J. Conroy, an international specialist with the law firm Baker & McKenzie in New York, crammed five Asian and European cities into a ten-day trip.

Conroy tries to segregate his trips into two-week chunks every six weeks, to produce long stretches of home time. He also takes advantage of odd hours of free time. He turned up at his office at 5:30 A.M. so he could spend afternoon hours with his daughter before his evening plane to Europe.

Ian Donnelly, CEO of Flexmaster in suburban Toronto, finds his international chimney products work taking him back to the Ould Sod. His advice: "To prevent jet lag: Go to sleep a couple of hours earlier (traveling east) or a couple of hours later (traveling west) for a few nights before your trip. The more time zones you cross, the more severe the problem." He adds: "First class is worth the additional cost—more room to work and more room to think."

East-West Continental Differences

A component of new globalization is the frequent shift of managers from east to west—or vice versa—within the United States. This 3,000-mile relocation requires as *much* getting used to (*more*, some say) than a New York to Frankfurt move.

The biggest difference: the ways East and West view time priorities. Executives who've worked both coasts say Westerners, who enjoy temperate climates, take more of the *mañana* attitude. They do spend more time enjoying themselves than do Easterners, driven indoors as they are six months of the year.

Further, East Coasters have little reverence for sleep—as Cheryl Heuton Falacci discovered when she flew the red-eye to New York for a meeting. Ignoring her protests that she needed time to nap, conference organizers scheduled her first meeting an hour after tarmac touchdown.

Falacci, who later changed her base to New York, says her new colleagues are equally demanding. Evening meetings, rare in Long Beach, California, are *de rigueur* in New York. One colleague, Falacci recalls, was curtly turned down when he asked for compensation time off to make up for overtime on a special project. Instead, managers told him to plan work hours so he "wouldn't feel as though" he needed time off.

Perhaps most difficult for transplanted Westerners is the East Coast insistence on hell-or-high-water punctuality. When Falacci arrived late at a Manhattan meeting because her subway stalled for 20 minutes between stops, her conferrers were frosty despite her explanation. "On the West Coast," she says, "you can walk in and say, 'I was stuck in this horrible traffic' and people sympathize."

Despite these changes, Falacci is hardly frazzled. Back in Long Beach, she spent most of her free time stuck in traffic. Her 20 miles to work took an hour. Grocery shopping, figuring in driving and parking, could take two hours. Eating out: all evening. But in Manhattan, restaurants and delivery services abound. Moviegoing can be planned in minutes. Grocery shopping is a breeze: "Just swing in the store on the same block, grab something, and you're out in ten minutes," Falacci marvels.

Falacci has maintained her West Coast fascination with rock climbing. In Long Beach, she and her husband drove 45 minutes to go climbing. But now they climb together two or three times a week in Central Park.

So, for eastern or western transplants, changes are needed. Easterners need to understand: Many Westerners consider themselves on time when they're only 15 minutes late and rarely act frantic even when pressured. Westerners need to appreciate a time commitment as literal—not as a casual target.

Time management, like other branches of administrative science, depends to some extent on where you're living and working—at the moment, that is.

NOTES

NOTES

NOTES

NOTES